VIBRANT FAITH

CHRIS GOLDMAN

HEARTSPRING PUBLISHING · JOPLIN, MISSOURI

Copyright © 2007
HeartSpring Publishing
www.heartspringpublishing.com
A division of College Press Publishing Co.

Toll-free order line 800-289-3300
On the web at www.collegepress.com

The 3:16 Series (Colossians 3:16)
"Let the word of Christ dwell in you richly . . . ."

Cover design by Brett Lyerla
Interior design by Dan Rees

International Standard Book Number 978-0-89900-496-9

HEARTSPRING'S
3:16 SERIES

The Apostle Paul encouraged Christians in the first century and therefore us today to "**allow the Word of Christ to dwell in us richly**" (Colossians 3:16, *NIV*).

The 3:16 Series is based on this verse in Colossians. The series is designed primarily for small group study and interaction but will also prove fruitful for individual study. Each participant is encouraged to read the chapter before the group's meeting. The interaction questions are designed to be the focal point of your group's discussion time.

Psalm 119:11 says, *"I have hidden Your Word in my heart that I might not sin against You."* One noteworthy feature of this series is that each study includes a suggested memory verse (a short verse or two from the passage that is being studied). A sheet of these has been included at the back of the book for you to take these verses with you wherever you go and refer to them throughout your day.

The HeartSpring Publishing website will continually be updated with small group ideas and tips to further enhance your study of each New Testament book in the 3:16 series. Be sure to log on to www.heartspringpublishing.com (College Press) frequently!

"**Let the Word of Christ . . . have the run of the house.
Give it plenty of room in your lives.**"
(Col. 3:16 *The Message*)

PREVIEWING OUR STUDY OF JAMES

CHRIS GOLDMAN

Have you ever been misunderstood? It is one of the most frustrating occurrences in life. You try to say one thing and people hear another. You try to get out the right words and the wrong ones escape. James is often misunderstood. Martin Luther wrote:

> In a word, St. John's Gospel and his first Epistle, St. Paul's Epistles, especially Romans, Galatians and Ephesians, and St. Peter's first Epistle are the books that show you Christ and teach you all that is necessary and good for you to know, even though you were never to see or hear any other book or doctrine. Therefore *St. James' Epistle is really an epistle of straw, compared to them; for it has nothing of the nature of the Gospel about it*.

True, James does not write about the cross or grace or mention the word "gospel." But you do not have to mention those things if you live them. That is what James's letter is all about—living according to the gospel you believe. Luther fought works-based religion that led many away from faith and placed legalism before love and faith, so it is easy to see why Luther shied away from James's practical lessons for the Christian life. James knew the Author of grace—Jesus Christ—personally and wrote to people who had come to know God's grace. He wrote to answer the question of faith lived out, not to answer questions on faith itself.

Over the centuries followers of Christ have troubled over balancing two key issues: grace and Christian living. Some see Paul and James as disagreeing over these two concepts. After all, Paul wrote about grace and James wrote about works. If we are saved by grace and not by works, then Paul and James must be at odds. This has led some down the road of what Bonhoeffer called cheap grace:

Cheap grace is the deadly enemy of our Church. We are fighting today for costly grace. Cheap grace means grace as a doctrine, a principle, a system. It means forgiveness of sins proclaimed as a general truth, the love of God taught as the Christian "conception" of God. . . .

Cheap grace means the justification of sin without the justification of the sinner. Grace alone does everything they say, and so everything can remain as it was before. "All for sin could not atone." Well, then, let the Christian live like the rest of the world, let him model himself on the world's standards in every sphere of life, and not presumptuously aspire to live a different life under grace from his old life under sin.

If we are saved by grace (and nothing we do can change that), then can we live any way we want? Paul's answer: "What shall we say, then? Shall we go on sinning so that grace may increase? By no means! We died to sin; how can we live in it any longer?" (Rom 6:1-2). The Apostle Paul explained grace through his letters to the Romans and Galatians; however, he understood that some would interpret grace as "cheap" and live any way they chose.

James wants to talk to us about faith and action, not grace and salvation. It is not that he opposes the ideas (a laughable thought), but because he understands the cost of grace more than most. James was, after all, the half-brother of Jesus Christ. He saw him grow up and knew Jesus in a way that only family can. He saw his brother who, from childhood, "had to be about his Father's business."

We must be careful to balance grace and Christian acts of service or we may end up with dangerous thoughts and beliefs. For example, we might find ourselves convinced our actions prove that our hearts are right with God. This is not true; it is possible to simply go through the motions of Christian living without any belief at all. Another dangerous thought that may emerge is that my faith is strong enough to eliminate the need for structured activity. In other words, the solidity of my belief removes my need to do what Jesus commanded in order to know that I am right with God. These kinds of thoughts gave birth to James's statement, "Faith without works is dead."

Understanding James requires good listening skills and careful attention to what he does not say in order to determine what he does say. Many think they hear James saying, "You are saved by what you do." For example, I might begin to think, "If I take care of widows and orphans, I am fine with God, and my moral weaknesses have no bearing on my faith." Others may walk away with a feeling of remorse. Their feelings are similar to

Understanding James requires good listening skills and careful attention to what he does not say.

the guilt felt by children whose dads tell them they will never measure up. We can know that James does not say these things based on one simple fact: he never says these things. People read between the lines and read the wrong ideas into James's writing. I would suggest that in reading James we would do better just to read the lines.

James demands that we back up our faith with action. This is not so we can be saved; it is because we *have been* saved. It is because we've been "bought with a price" and our bodies are not our own. It is because we have decided to, "deny our self[ves], take up our cross[es] and follow Jesus." In other words, James writes to a people who are already saved; he just wants to challenge believers to respond like they really believe their salvation.

We need to give James a fair hearing, clear our minds of the stereotypical approaches, and simply sit and listen to a man who, over the centuries, has often been misunderstood.

TABLE OF CONTENTS

VIBRANT FAITH

CHAPTER ONE

RISING TO PERFECTION

JAMES 1:1-12

Long's Peak rises above the Colorado clouds, towering over Estes Park at an elevation of 14,259 feet above sea level. Climbing from Estes Park to the Peak was part of my life for three consecutive summers. Growing up on the high desert of southeastern New Mexico, this beautiful country had an amazing effect on my life. Even though we trekked five miles during the middle of July, snow blanketed the mountains and the sound of the cold rushing springs filled the high-country air.

One year as we approached Chasm Lake, which rests four miles above the ranger station, we were treated to the sight of an eagle flying below us. It rode the mountain air with such grace and perfection. The eagle in flight is one of my pictures of perfection. The promise of Isaiah echoed in my mind as I took in the moment, ". . . but those who hope in the LORD will renew their strength. They will soar on wings like eagles; they will run and not grow weary, they will walk and not be faint" (Isa 40:31).

James opens his letter to the faithful with these words of encouragement and a call to rise above:

> Consider it pure joy, my brothers, whenever you face trials of many kinds, because you know that the testing of your faith develops perseverance. Perseverance must finish its work *so that you may be mature and complete, not lacking anything* (Jas 1:2-4, emphasis mine).

"Mature and complete, not lacking anything." I like the sound of that. If my spiritual walk with God could rise to that level, soaring on wings like eagles wouldn't seem so distant. Many people I talk to don't feel like soaring eagles, they feel more like grounded 747s. We want to rise up and fly but feel overcommitted to our daily routine and under-committed to our walk with God.

Spiritual maturity refers to a wholeness that most of us rarely experience. If asked, "Is your walk with God lacking anything?" the most common answer would be a resounding "Yes!" In the original language, these words—maturity, complete, lacking nothing—convey a similar idea to Jesus' words in Matthew 5:48, "Be perfect, therefore, as your heavenly Father is perfect." The ancient Aramaic language had a word *tamim* that is the grandfather of these words in the Greek language. It means to be "wholly given." God knows that none of us can be perfect (without fault). Jesus' words when he calls his followers to be perfect are confusing because of the way we think of perfection. If we translated it this way, "Be wholly given to God as God is wholly given to you," it makes more sense. We understand the idea of being completely invested in something, one hundred percent committed. We also understand that a person can be one hundred percent committed and still make mistakes. Being wholly given to God—being mature and lacking nothing—is really what we all desire.

But how do we get there? How do we rise above and spiritually take flight? James's answer is a mixed bag. The "joy" part sounds inviting, but the trials and testing sound like something to avoid. And yet, what they produce is what I want. It's what I desire for my walk with God. So where do we start?

The starting point for James is counting our blessings each day. The old Christian hymn, "Count Your Blessings" comes to mind. "Count your blessings; name them one by one. . . . Count your many blessings, see what God has done." For some reason when I sang that as a child I was thinking of warmth, shelter, clothing, food, money, comfort. I wasn't thinking of trials, tests, and perseverance. We are called to reframe these as opportunities for growth and not obstacles in the way of happiness.

> The starting point for James is counting our blessings each day.

We need to begin our daily walk with God counting our blessings that come from . . . well, from anywhere. This includes the good and the bad, the comfortable and uncomfortable. A friend of mine, Bonnie, taught me this. She sat in a wheelchair unable to move her legs for several years. One day I got up the courage to ask what had happened. She was working and making money in the heart of Silicon Valley when one day she woke up paralyzed.

My heart and sympathy went out to her until she told me one of the more remarkable statements of faith I've ever heard: she claimed it was a gift that had moved her from self-reliance to God-reliance in just a matter of weeks. What would have torn away any faith in most people brought faith into her life. What would have caused many to turn their backs on God caused her to look for God for the first time in her life.

Blessings come in all kinds of shapes and sizes. If we're not looking for them, we miss them. We miss the blessed thorn in the flesh that Paul learned to appreciate when he said:

> To keep me from becoming conceited because of these surpassingly great revelations, there was given me a thorn in my flesh, a messenger of Satan, to torment me. Three times I pleaded with the Lord to take it away from me. But he said to me, "My grace is sufficient for you, for my power is made perfect in weakness." Therefore I will boast all the more gladly about my weaknesses, so that Christ's power may rest on me. That is why, for Christ's sake, I delight in weaknesses, in insults, in hardships, in persecutions, in difficulties. For when I am weak, then I am strong (2 Cor 12:7-10).

It's the difference between Job and his wife. Job looked to God because of the trials. His wife cursed God because of the trials. James wants us to have the faith of Paul, Job, and Bonnie. It would do us good to say, "God, thanks for the pain. I'm experiencing great joy because of this trial."

The starting point for rising to this level of wholeness is a change of perspective on tests and trials. Once we change our perspective, we can begin to understand what James is trying to get us to see: tests and trials increase spiritual productivity. Maturity is a direct byproduct of faithfully passing the tests and trials of life.

Another benefit is the effect on our prayer life. You want to see a person who believes in the power of prayer? You'll find it under the rock of burden and suffering before you find it on top of the cushion of comfortable living. Our wealth has sucked the richness out of our prayer life. Faith that believes in prayer enough to ask God for wisdom is faith that has been strengthened through obstacles. Faith that asks without doubting is faith that's held on to hope through struggles and knows that God is present, especially in the tough times.

> Once we change our perspective, we can begin to understand what James is trying to get us to see

In the course of a few months two families in the church where I preach lost twenty-year-old daughters to drunk drivers. They were stolen from life. People asked some really tough questions during those months. "Why did God do this to these families?" "How could he let this happen?" "What was his plan? What's he trying to accomplish with this?" My answer is nothing. God didn't cause it to happen; God didn't want it to happen. God doesn't work that way. However, he can do an amazing thing with Satan-induced tragedy: He can bring about faith that is tested, tried, and refined.

Peter wrote about this when he said, "In this you greatly rejoice, though now for a little while you may have had to suffer grief in all kinds of trials. These have come so that your faith—of greater worth than gold, which perishes even though refined by fire—may be proved genuine and may result in praise, glory and honor when Jesus Christ is revealed" (1 Pet 1:6-7).

Here's this mixed bag again. The Apostles seemed more likely to attach thanks to suffering than to wealth. In our culture, we are most likely to attach thanks to wealth rather than to suffering—unless it's thanks for suffering done *for us*, not *by us*.

Most of us who live in modern cultures have been acclimated to luxury leading to our own demise. Consider this: if Jesus said, "I tell you, it is easier for a camel to go through the eye of a needle than for a rich man to enter the kingdom of God" (Matt 19:24), why do we consider wealth as a blessing from Jesus and not an attack by Satan? We'll look at the other side of this coin in the next chapter, but for now it's a valid question to ask and a thought worth pondering.

Rethinking this matter helps us understand the upside-down world that James proposes. He imagines a world where the poor are proud because of their high position and the rich remember that they'll die just like the rest of us. He imagines a world where a poor person can smile in the face of poverty because of the wealth they have through faith in Christ. He imagines a world where wealthy people utilize their funds for God and people around them because they can't take it with them . . . and they live like it! It's a world where a wealthy Silicon Valley worker wakes up unable to walk and says, "Thanks, God, for the new direction in life."

Blessings, blessings, and more blessings are revealed because of the trials, tests, and long-suffering. I love James's insistence on this point. "Blessed is the man who perseveres under trial, because when he has stood the test, he will receive the crown of life that God has promised to those who love him" (Jas 1:12).

This is exactly where I see James in line with the good news of Jesus Christ and his teachings. The famous beatitudes from the Sermon on the Mount are Jesus' statements calling his disciples to see the blessings that we miss because they're disguised as curses and marketed as such by the world around us. Even the Hebrew writer sees this when it comes to the suffering of Christ, "Let us fix our eyes on Jesus, the author and perfecter of our faith, *who for the joy set before him* endured the cross, scorning its shame, and sat down at the right hand of the throne of God" (Heb 12:2, emphasis mine). Suffering is seen as a source of blessing and joy because of the place we take with God when we've made it through to the other side.

What Am I Supposed to Ask For?

The opening of James makes me take a step back and really think about my prayer life. I've known about asking for wisdom. I've meditated on asking without doubts. I've realized that my lack of faith is overshadowed by God's faithfulness. But I've never ever wanted to offer a prayer that says, "God, send me some trials and tests because I want to grow in my relationship with you, and it's just been too comfortable for me."

> My lack of faith is overshadowed by God's faithfulness.

Growing up, my family was friends with the Kramer family. They were missionaries from South America who dropped in once every few years. When they were coming, we'd sit by the window for hours (it seemed) hoping to see their VW minibus round the corner and head to our house. They always seemed happy and full of life. What they did then—driving across the country with eight children and two parents—they couldn't do today because of current seatbelt laws.

The Kramers had a theory in life: never own anything you can't leave behind. They often had to return to the States while things in South America calmed down politically. While waiting, they set up temporary shop in American society and waited for the doors to open once again. When the doors opened to return to a world of poverty and discomfort, they gladly walked out the door, leaving the "stuff" behind and taking only what they really needed.

My problem is that I seek to set up a permanent shop—nothing temporary about it. In my shop, I want every kind of creature comfort money can afford and every convenience I can convince myself is really a necessity. I find myself not "wholly given" to God but completely owned by my stuff. My possessions also serve another purpose in my life: to prevent any trials and tests that might distract me from comfortable living.

While I'm caught in a spiritual battle, I'm also caught in a cultural battle. The American culture demands that personal comfort and ease be a high priority in life. When anything threatens our comfort, we fight back with money, cars, convenience, technology, medications, and on and on it goes. This mentality was best shown in one of my son's favorite childhood movies, *Hook*. In it, Robin Williams plays Peter Pan, now married and far removed from Neverland. Captain Hook has crossed into the real world to steal his children in order to induce the final showdown between the two. In one dramatic scene, he demands that Peter fight. In response, the out-of-shape and financially dependent Peter pulls out a check book and asks, "How much? Name your price." Hook doesn't want money, in his words, "I want my war!"

> Money cannot buy immortality or even promise satisfaction in daily living.

Humanity has always believed that more money can solve everything. James reminds us that money cannot buy immortality and can't even promise satisfaction in daily living. So if you're poor, be pleased with your high position. This message is similar to Solomon's message in Ecclesiastes:

> Whoever loves money never has money enough; whoever loves wealth is never satisfied with his income. . . . As goods increase, so do those who consume them. And what benefit are they to the owner except to feast his eyes on them? The sleep of a laborer is sweet, whether he eats little or much, but the abundance of a rich man permits him no sleep (Eccl 5:10-12).

You can never have enough money if that's what you live for. You can never buy enough of anything to satisfy those who consume everything. You can never do more with possessions than simply admire the fact that you have them. But what would you pay for a good night's sleep? Solomon suggests that the poor laborer has something to be happy about—he sleeps soundly at night because his labor forces rest. The rich man, on the other hand, can't sleep because he's constantly worried about all of his possessions, businesses, crops, money, etc.

James and Solomon give similar words of encouragement that come from completely different motivations. Solomon, "Be happy because you can sleep." James, "Be happy because of the wealth you have through Jesus Christ." While the former may be a reason to smile and motivate you through the day, the latter is a reason to rejoice and smile in the face of poverty.

Where the World Lives

The world pursues material happiness like it is the carrot dangling in front of them. They consider themselves blessed when they have more, eat more, and buy more. We consider prosperity and fame synonymous with blessings and wisdom. James gets in the face of these American cultural norms and says, "Think again! Count your blessings and try starting with the blessings you casually confuse as burdens." With this mind-set we will actually get what we want and receive something that will actually satisfy: wholeness in the Lord and a satisfied existence that is lacking nothing. 3:16

Rising to Perfection 1

Rising to Perfection

1. If you were promised the ability to purchase spiritual maturity and wholeness in your relationship with God (guaranteed), what price would you be willing to pay? According to James, what is the price for spiritual growth and maturity?

2. Wisdom is the ability to apply knowledge at the appropriate time and in the appropriate place. James says if you want wisdom, ask God and he'll give it to you. However, he doesn't say how God will deliver it. Do you think there is a connection between God's wisdom and daily tests and trials?

3. We tend to believe that our next purchase will be the one that brings joy and satisfaction. When was the last time you bought something that truly brought you satisfaction in life? When was the last time something or someone in life gave you a sense of contentment?

4. Why is it equally difficult for the poor to take pride in their position of honor and the rich to take pride in their humble situation? What tends to get in the way of both the rich and poor?

5. What experiences in life have helped you to grow and mature in your relationship with God and others? Share with your group or family one tough experience you've faced that has really turned out to be a blessing in your life.

Memory Verse James 1:2-4

Consider it pure joy, my brothers, whenever you face trials of many kinds, because you know that the testing of your faith develops perseverance. Perseverance must finish its work so that you may be mature and complete, not lacking anything.

CHAPTER TWO

"GOOD FROM ABOVE"

JAMES 1:12-21

Science fiction writers ignite my imagination with stories of mind implants. Books and movies cover the gamut with stories about erasing the mind, blocking the mind, calming the mind, and sometimes enhancing it. Implanting detailed knowledge of martial arts is the concept of one movie. Another suggests the ability to see what will happen through seeing into the minds of others who see into the future. While tampering with the mind makes me nervous, the suggested benefits are—I have to admit—enticing.

How great would it be to get a brain implant from God? To have instant, on-demand knowledge of God's will would seem to clear up a lot of problems. People wouldn't have to wear WWJD bracelets because they would instantly know the answer to the question, "What would Jesus do?" The information would be on their minds right as it is needed. Downloading the entire Bible through a brain implant would be another place to start. Or what about a concordance that could work in your mind like it does on a computer?

If science fiction stories predict future technology, perhaps one day we'll be able to download a Bible degree instantly instead of spending years studying, reading, and writing. Of course there's a problem with this idea: a lack of knowledge isn't my only problem in life. Wisdom is really the issue. Wisdom is the ability to apply knowledge in the right way at the right time. You can't download that—you learn it. You develop it over time by facing life's trials and temptations.

Recently I had a discussion with a frustrated Christian studying James in class. She felt that the entire class was pushing for people to live perfectly in every situation. Every week she left feeling guilty and unworthy because the bar had been set so high that she couldn't rise to the level of Christian living that pleases the Lord.

James knows better and isn't suggesting that you can live a sin-free life. He knows that no one except Jesus could live without sin. His issue isn't living a sin-free life. It's more about living an effort-free life, something that many of us get caught doing. We find ourselves existing in faith without giving an honest effort to apply what we know. We try to live knowledge-filled (really information-overloaded) and wisdom-empty lives.

Some of the wisest advice I ever received had to do with moral situations that tend to compromise our faith. The advice was to make the decision on Sunday what you're going to do Friday. In other words, don't wait for the temptation to blindside you; decide ahead of time how you're going to escape. Making a decision under duress is unnecessarily difficult.

Don't wait for the temptation to blindside you.

It's interesting to me that wisdom under pressure is how James opens up his letter. He knows that when trials and tests come, a person needs to have wisdom to navigate through the tough stuff. He continues this line of thought as he writes:

> Blessed is the man who perseveres under trial, because when he has stood the test, he will receive the crown of life that God has promised to those who love him.
> When tempted, no one should say, "God is tempting me." For God cannot be tempted by evil, nor does he tempt anyone; but each one is tempted when, by his own evil desire, he is dragged away and enticed. Then, after desire has conceived, it gives birth to sin; and sin, when it is full-grown, gives birth to death (1:12-15).

James knows that we can't live sin free. He also knows that by nature, Christians shouldn't live effort-free. He knows we can all do better.

Spiritually, all of the Apostles make sure we know that we're in a spiritual battle. The enemy is attacking with one purpose in mind: destruction. This is the nature of war. You don't fight a war to hold the enemy at bay. You fight to win. This is what makes wars like Vietnam and Iraq so difficult. The enemy only has one way to have any level of victory—get the opposition to give up and go home.

The battle that we're fighting is part of a war that's already been won. The enemy can't win; he can only hope to keep attacking and countering for so long that we give up and go home. He can't win by conquering us; he can only win by fueling our own desire to retreat.

It's a spiritual battle between the kingdom of light and the kingdom of darkness.

These two kingdoms are very different. One is a kingdom of conviction, belief, faith wisdom, resolve, victory, and life. The kingdom of darkness is one of compromise, distrust, the physically tangible, knowledge, tolerance, spiritual defeat, and death without hope.

In our battle, James wants us to understand what we're experiencing. Satan tempts and God tests. These are very different. As a matter of fact they are so distinct that James draws a clear line in the sand: God cannot and will not tempt.

The word "test" in James literally means trials. Nobody likes tests. Tests are given in school so a student can demonstrate what he or she has learned. You need trials and should be thankful for them according to James. Why? Because, like a test in school, a trial forces you to apply what you know; forces you to demonstrate wisdom. God tests or disciplines those he loves like children (see Heb 12:7-11).

I wish all tests could be like the SAT test. Take it over and over and the colleges will take your highest score in each of the three categories. If only all school tests could've been like that. Most tests don't have any grace built into them at all. The SAT test is one of the few with a chance to take it again and do it better. The tests that God gives through every-day life are similar—except He takes it a step further and guarantees a positive outcome for us. This is because our success depends on God's accomplishments rather than our own accomplishments. So why do we still have to take the test?

Trials and tests can come from God and have a benefit for us. They help us mature and rise to perfection, which is wholeness in God. The good news is that tests are provided by everyday life free of charge in unlimited quantities! The opportunity for growth is infinite. As a matter of fact, we don't need to generate or manufacture trials because, as Jesus said, "Each day has enough trouble of its own" (Matt 6:34).

> **Tests are provided by everyday life free of charge in unlimited quantities.**

Temptations are different. Temptations begin when we are seduced by our own desires. We want something. We desire someone. We become seduced by what we can't have, and this leads to sin. James is very practical about the issue. Tests are from God; temptations are a partnership between our lust and Satan's strategic attack on God's people.

In the thriller movie, *Silence of the Lambs*, the serial killer, Hannibal Lector, makes a profound observation. He is assisting an FBI agent to catch a serial killer who has avoided arrest. In a desperate attempt to understand the killer, the authorities go to a killer in order to solve the crime. He gives them an insight into human nature: killers covet what they know before taking what they don't know. In other words, we are tempted not by what we don't see; we are tempted by what we see every day.

Think about the tenth commandment, "You shall not covet your neighbor's wife" (Exod 20:17). Why your neighbor's wife? Because your neighbor's wife is what you see every day in the course of living. God knows what our weakness is: we see something we can't have or shouldn't have, and suddenly we have to have it. It's the car just out of reach, the house just a little more luxurious, the position that would make our lives a little more powerful. . . . It's the tree in the middle of the garden. We see, we want, we take, we sin, we destroy, we suffer, and we are ruined. We are enticed by the forbidden.

Satan uses this nature of ours against us. His strategy is plain for all to see. He desires to lure us from the kingdom of conviction into the kingdom of compromise. He accomplishes this by using our eyes and desires. We see sexual satisfaction, material possessions, political power, or the opportunity to get even and are drawn out of the light into the darkness.

We think it's just a short walk back, but we forget that we often get trapped in the darkness because we can't see the way home.

The difference between God's tests and Satan's temptations could be illustrated by the differences between boot camp and battle. Most people remember what they were doing on September 11, 2001, when the World Trade Center was attacked. I remember virtually every detail about that day. Our friend Jenni was scheduled to leave for boot camp the week of September 11, 2001. Joining the military took on a whole new meaning that day for everyone who had enlisted. We watched the TV and sat shell-shocked by what we saw. The implications for every person in the military weighed heavily on everyone's hearts.

Her departure was delayed for about a week before she reported to boot camp. When her training was completed, we were allowed to see some video footage of the training. It included clips of simulated attacks, as well as real encounters with guns and bombs. We watched graphic scenes of the soldiers walking through a building filled with a gas—only the soldiers were without gas masks. Day by day the soldiers were torn down and retrained. I didn't see one enjoyable moment or exercise. As a matter of fact, there was nothing she experienced that made me desire the experience of military training.

The purpose of boot camp is to save lives when soldiers are faced with a real battle. Through the training and simulations, the military knows soldiers have a better chance of surviving a real battle.

Battle is very different from boot camp. In a battle the attacks come from the hands of a deadly enemy, not a drill instructor. The enemy may use the same guns and gases that you saw in boot camp, but now they are being used for one purpose: destruction. Sometimes we forget the difference between the two. According to James we should be filled with joy when we face trials and stand up under the pressure. Just as boot camp trains soldiers, trials help us become mature and strong. However, don't make the mistake of facing a temptation and thinking that God is tempting you. Temptations are the battlefield of our enemy. Temptations aren't from God and don't have any purpose other than destruction. Can we be strengthened by standing strong in the face of temptation? Yes. But this is a self-induced threat that is aided and abetted by Satan who wants to see us compromised and destroyed.

Temptations are conceived in our hearts, give birth to sin, and end in destruction. James uses an illustration we can identify with to describe temptation and sin. He uses the life cycle. We are conceived,

> Sometimes we forget the difference between battle and boot camp.

born, live, and then die. Temptation is conceived by desire. It gives birth to sin. Then as the sin matures, we discover that only death and destruction can come from the sin.

As people we are concerned where thoughts, ideas, and feelings come from. We internalize these issues and process them in our hearts and minds. James knows this and gives us insight into the origination of sin, trials, struggles, etc. However, tests aren't the only things that originate with God. James continues:

> Don't be deceived, my dear brothers. Every good and perfect gift is from above, coming down from the Father of the heavenly lights, who does not change like shifting shadows. He chose to give us birth through the word of truth, that we might be a kind of firstfruits of all he created (1:16-18).

God is also the clear source of every good and perfect gift. Many are hesitant to take this approach. The thinking is, "If God gets credit for everything good, then he also has to take responsibility for everything bad." James wants to prevent this kind of thinking. God is the source of good—blessings and tests. Satan is the source of evil—temptations and sin.

Solutions and Considerations

We need to discipline ourselves to remember the *origin* of tests, trials, and temptations. We also need to remember the origin of the good and perfect blessings we receive. James states emphatically that every good and perfect gift comes from God.

Over the years I've known many people who are uncomfortable with Christians who give God credit for every good thing that happens in their lives. According to James, we might want to be uncomfortable with their discomfort. If it's good, give God the credit. If it's a test, it might be from God. If it's a trial, keep God with you and face it with faith. If it's a temptation, don't blame that on God. Don't allow the temptation to give birth to sin and destruction.

He then approaches a subject that seems at first glance disassociated from the discussion of tests, trials, and temptations:

> My dear brothers, take note of this: Everyone should be quick to listen, slow to speak and slow to become angry, for man's anger does not bring about the righteous life that God desires. Therefore, get rid of all moral filth and the evil that is so prevalent and humbly accept the word planted in you, which can save you (1:19-21).

These words are directly connected with the discussion of sin and temptations. One of our temptations is to correct our behavior and the behavior of others through anger. James makes it clear that anger doesn't produce righteousness. It doesn't lead to righteousness in our life or the lives of others.

Wisdom would dictate that we listen and learn in an effort to avoid the destruction. Listen to the word of truth that gives birth to life. Listen to the faith that doesn't falter in the face of the enemy. Only through this can you put aside the immorality that continues to ruin the lives of so many.

Listening to the word of truth takes me back to the desire for a brain implant of God's Word. The truth is that we have the truth implanted in our minds and on our hearts. God planted—literally implanted—His word in our lives and it leads to salvation. How this works I'm not exactly sure. But this I do know, God's word is living—it's not just known. I can know historical facts. I can know algebraic equations. But God's word lives in us, and it is active. The problem isn't knowledge of God's word or the power of God's word, the problem is a shortage of wisdom. It's the ability to apply the knowledge we have during a trial or at the point of temptation. We have the word, but we don't listen to the word or allow the word to dwell in our hearts like we should.

Solomon describes the way we need to listen to God's word and keep it close to us:

> My son, obey your father's commands
>   and do not forsake your mother's teaching.
> Bind them upon your heart forever;
>   fasten them around your neck.
> When you walk, they will guide you;
>   when you sleep, they will watch over you;
>   when you awake, they will speak to you.
> For these commands are a lamp,
>   this teaching is a light,
> and the corrections of discipline
>   are the way to life . . . (Prov 6:20-23).

The words of our Father should be kept in our hearts and surrounding our lives. They are a counselor leading us in life. They provide protection in the darkness of night when we are vulnerable as we sleep. They are a trusted advisor when we wake in the morning. They are light when we walk into a dark world. The discipline of the Lord and any tests He may put us through lead us not just *through* life . . . they lead us *to* life!

Don't make the mistake of confusing where good things come from: they all come from God. Don't make the mistake of confusing where

> The tests the Lord may put us through lead us not just through life but to life!

temptations come from: they all come from deep within our desires fueled by Satan. Don't avoid tests and trials: they can help you grow. As a matter of fact it is through the trials and tests that we develop vibrant faith. 3:16

24

✝

C
H
A
P
T
E
R

2   *"Good from Above"*

Rising to Perfection

1. When a trial or test comes your way, do you find yourself embracing it as a blessing or running away from it as a curse?

2. The ability to recognize whether you're going through a test, trial, or temptation is important for our spiritual walk with God. Sometimes it can be difficult to identify which is which. Take a moment to do just that. Consider the last month of your life and identify (as best you can) one test, one trial, and one temptation that has challenged your life.

   Test (sent by God to strengthen your faith or discipline you as his child)

   Trial (struggles in life that challenge every person)

   Temptation (generated by your own desires and gives birth to sin)

3. When you consider James's statement that, ". . . every good and perfect gift comes from above," how does that shape the way you pray to God on a daily basis? How is it a statement of faith to give God credit for every blessing that comes your way?

4. Write down a few specific ways that God's Word can be "implanted" on your mind and heart.

5. What is the advantage of allowing the Word to "dwell in you richly"?

Memory Verse
James 1:19-20

My dear brothers, take note of this: Everyone should be quick to listen, slow to speak and slow to become angry, for man's anger does not bring about the righteous life that God desires.

CHAPTER THREE

PLAYING FAVORITES

JAMES 1:27–2:13

Pe*eople have a tendency to take care of their own kind. It's a fact. We naturally have an inclination to gravitate toward the familiar. This may be why Sunday is still considered the most segregated day of the week in American culture. We can choose to go anywhere we like, and yet we often choose to assemble where people are just like us.

Working in a church in Northern California that has been blessed with many generations and ethnicities, I'm keenly aware when I'm away from home. A few years ago I visited a church in the Bible belt with some friends. I was stunned at how "white" the audience was. Not that there's a problem with a group of white people getting together for worship, but stunned because the city where the church was located wasn't ethnically represented. After services I decided to ask about the situation and was informed that in fact they were seeking to overcome the problem and were the primary supporters for an African-American congregation located in the downtown neighborhoods.

I want to be culturally careful here. Planting a church in a neighborhood to make it easy and convenient for people to attend worship right where they live is a good thing. However, looking at a community where everyone has a car and it only takes 15 minutes to drive from one end of town to the other, I wonder if it's the right approach for this community.

That same year I was invited to teach a class at a convention that is dominantly attended by African-American Christians and organized by African-American churches. It saddened me when I learned that this convention had been in existence for more than 50 years and I'd never heard about it. My family and I were well received and everyone took note of us—and I do mean took note. We walked in Wednesday night and—as is my custom—I insisted that we sit toward the front where the singing tends to encourage me the most.

To get this picture, you must know that my entire family is about as white as white people get—fair skin, blonde hair. As we walked into the convention center which was packed with 3,000 in attendance, every head turned and watched this family who made its way to the front. When we had to leave, several of our members who are African-American caught us in the hall and assured us how proud they were to see their minister in attendance. They also noticed the absence of those who chose not to come.

These two illustrations tell us something about human nature: We tend to flock with the familiar. We tend to take care of our own. We tend towards comfort and the usual rather than stretching ourselves past discomfort. We tend to play favorites.

> We tend to flock with the familiar. We tend to take care of our own.

James hits this subject head on:

> Religion that God our Father accepts as pure and faultless is this: to look after orphans and widows in their distress and to keep oneself from being polluted by the world.
>
> My brothers, as believers in our glorious Lord Jesus Christ, don't show favoritism. Suppose a man comes into your meeting wearing a gold ring and fine clothes, and a poor man in shabby clothes also comes in. If you show special attention to the man wearing fine clothes and say, "Here's a good seat for you," but say to the poor man, "You stand there" or "Sit on the floor by my feet," have you not discriminated among yourselves and become judges with evil thoughts? (1:27–2:4).

It's almost as if James were written more for our culture than for the first-century church. Think about what we pursue. We tend to pursue religious living more than faithful living. We have so many churches in our world that the world can't see or hear the testimony of the church. Why so many churches? So we can clump together with the clan that is most like us or is most likely to promote our preferences. This allows us to be around people like us. This allows us to take care of our own kind.

God cuts through the religious rhetoric and spells it out clearly for us. Real religion that is respected by God is the care and meaningful concern for those who aren't in the mainstream. It's faithful living that brings the marginalized back into the center—back into the center of the church's concern.

In the book *Under the Overpass*, Mike Yankoski and his friend Sam leave upper-middle-class suburbia and live on the streets for five months. It's not an experiment for Mike—it's a test of his faith. A test he needed to pass in order to know if his faith was real.[1]

As you read about their encounters with the streets, you are also treated to a new perspective of the church world. This is the faith adventure of two university students who are studying theology and computer science . . . and studying human nature. One week they are accepted and welcomed, the next they are questioned and considered a threat.

One story they tell could have been inserted into James's text if they had lived when he wrote his letter. As on every Sunday, they try to locate a church nearby to attend. On this particular Sunday, they enter into a megachurch filming its own morning worship for worldwide distribution. The technology is everywhere in the building, the filming crews are in place, and security personnel are making sure everything goes off without a hitch. Mike can't handle the shock of going from the street into a multimillion dollar production known as the modern American church. As Mike slips into the bathroom to clean up, security guards begin to question him to determine if he was the same man who had charged the stage to disrupt the worship services just a few moments earlier. Mike assures them he's not the one who sought to disrupt the services. They skeptically watch Mike as he cleans himself up. He's clearly a person to keep their eye on. He was targeted as a potential problem.

Just a few months before, they would've been targeted, but not for security reasons. They would've been targeted as top-quality prospects. What changed? The heart or the mind or the soul? No. What changed was the clothes and living conditions.

James knows that God is concerned with what the world has forgotten. Brandy was, in a sense, forgotten by the world. When I worked in the Bay Area, she walked the same street as the church where I worked. More people on the streets knew her because of her short-shorts and halter tops.

Brandy was an example of the church behaving well. She walked into our lives by walking into one of the worship services. Every man's head turned and every woman's elbow went into action. It would've been easy for the looks and actions to send this woman on her way, But she'd seen enough of the street, and the women of the church knew that from just looking.

No doubt she was a distraction. She insisted on sitting front and center so she could take the entire service in. She obviously didn't have much money and certainly wasn't about to upgrade her clothes for worship. The ladies embraced her, took her shopping, and befriended her. I can't remember being more proud of God's people in action.

We play favorites in many ways. The wealthy often attend popular churches in order to make business contacts with other rich people who are potential sources of more wealth. Poor people often go to churches with poor people because they feel so out of place at other churches. Either way, it's people taking care of their own kind; gravitating towards "their own people." It's not what God intended for His church.

The "evil thoughts" James talks about are the thoughts we depend on to summarize a life by sizing it up externally. We see people's skin color and clothes style, listen to their words, determine their educational and materialistic value, and believe we've got them pegged. The problem? You can't peg someone without prejudging someone (prejudice). Prejudice is what leads to preferential treatment. Preferential treatment is based on the belief that we can see into a heart by glancing at the superficial.

James warns Christians not to do this. Don't assume anything about people, and don't allow externals to determine your treatment towards others. Treat widows and orphans with respect, honor, and love. Treat the poor man equally with the rich man. Why? Because the poor aren't so poor and the rich aren't so rich!

> Don't assume anything about people or allow externals to determine your treatment of them.

> Listen, my dear brothers: Has not God chosen those who are poor in the eyes of the world to be rich in faith and to inherit the kingdom he promised those who love him? But you have insulted the poor. Is it not the rich who are exploiting you? Are they not the ones who are dragging you into court? Are they not the ones who are slandering the noble name of him to whom you belong? (2:5-6).

God has blessed people who lack materialistic possessions with an understanding of faith and dependence that the rest of us often lack. Jesus stated this as well in the very first beatitude, "Blessed are the poor in spirit, for theirs is the kingdom of heaven" (Matt 5:3). Wealth brings independence and the belief that, "we've done pretty well for ourselves." The poor depend on God because they can't make it day to day without the hope of a better day.

James also points out something about the rich: the rich are usually the ones fighting against Christ and his church. It was true then, and it's true now. The poor are busy surviving. The political halls are filled with those who have enough food and plenty of possessions. This gives them time to concern themselves with issues that frankly shouldn't be of concern at all.

We see this in our culture today. It's the wealthy who invest their "expendable income" (I've always wondered how people have income they don't need) to remove God's name from money or the cross from cemeteries. James isn't assuming anti-Christian behavior on the part of the rich, he's simply pointing it out—he's stating the obvious. It doesn't mean that everyone of means is on the wrong side of the cross. It does mean, however, that you can't automatically assume good things because a person looks good, smells good, and gives good.

Living in California has been a great experience for me. I've met more cultures and classes than I dreamed existed. Every time we've looked for houses and neighborhoods, realtors are quick to give us demographic information about the neighborhood and schools. Why? People want to pick their neighbor. The problem is that a good neighbor can leave and be replaced by a bad tenant. You can't secure your neighbor.

Loving your neighbor is a key discipline of disciples:

> If you really keep the royal law found in Scripture, "Love your neighbor as yourself," you are doing right. But if you show favoritism, you sin and are convicted by the law as lawbreakers. For whoever keeps the whole law and yet stumbles at just one point is guilty of breaking all of it. For he who said, "Do not commit adultery," also said, "Do not murder." If you do not commit adultery but do commit murder, you have become a lawbreaker (2:8-10).

This is not to say if you commit one sin you might as well go all the way because there is no difference. Trust me, the consequences can be very different, and the consequences are what affect us most. Rather, the intention is to raise the level of respect we have towards others—especially the marginalized and the forgotten. Respect according to James isn't just theoretical. It's the way we think about people, the way we treat people, and the way we take care of people.

We categorize sins the same way we categorize people. One is worse than another. One is more offensive to God than another. This is how we often think. James wants to elevate the command to love people to a level of greater respect than it's given in the cultural mainstream; a level of respect that includes action. What he's getting at is this: treating your neighbor without love is no different than commit-

> Treating your neighbor without love is no better than adultery or murder.

ting adultery or murder. Really? Isn't that more than a little over the top?

Not really. James knew the teaching of Christ regarding murder and adultery. Christ stated, "But I tell you that anyone who is angry with his brother will be subject to judgment" (Matt 5:22). He also warned, "Anyone who looks at a woman lustfully has already committed adultery with her in his heart" (Matt 5:28). Both of these sins are best dealt with at the second command level, "Love your neighbor as yourself." True love for people moves us away from hate and lust. It moves us to look beyond the physical appeal.

The warning from James is sobering:

> Speak and act as those who are going to be judged by the law that gives freedom, because judgment without mercy will be shown to anyone who has not been merciful. Mercy triumphs over judgment! (2:12-13).

This sounds really positive and appealing: The judgment of mercy and freedom. "That's the kind of judgment I want," we think. James echoes Christ in the Lord's Prayer and states, "Then that's the kind of judgment you should practice" (see Matt 6:12).

Mercy does triumph over judgment. We shout praises when we receive mercy. Mercy is always desired but rarely given. The phrase, "You can dish it out but you can't take it," comes to mind except reversed. You can take mercy, but you can't dish it out. We like to judge others. We like to run people down, criticize them. It takes far less energy.

It is a rule of life: it's easier to tear down than to build up. When we moved into the Sacramento area, we lived behind the Birdcage Mall. It was an indoor-outdoor shopping venue with major department stores and a theater. It | **It's easier to tear down than to build up.**

had run down over the years and was scheduled for renovation. We knew that would improve the neighborhood and increase home values, so we moved in.

One day during my morning run I saw the wrecking crew arrive at the sight. Every day their work intrigued me . . . for three weeks. At the end of three weeks, the entire mall was completely gone. I was amazed how fast the buildings were destroyed and hauled off. Next came the renovations. The reconstruction started within the month and has continued until now—eight years later. Point: it's easier to tear down than to build up.

Mercy and freedom edify—they build people up. Judgment tears them down. Mercy is hard, judgment is easy. The disciple responding

‡

C
H
A
P
T
E
R

to James's teaching has decided not to base his Christian walk on works-based salvation; he is depending on mercy and freedom. Judgment leads to legalistic religion that depends on checklist Christianity. Mercy leads to freedom for all.

Mercy and grace, like any other gift, come with greater responsibility. James is only making the same argument made by Jesus and the other Apostles: The amazing gift of God's Son warrants a greater response. Not a response in order to be saved, but a response of freedom because you've already been saved. You've already experienced mercy beyond measure. Greater judgment will come upon the one who received mercy but specializes in merciless judgment for others. Jesus' parable of the unmerciful servant made this clear (see Matt 18:23-35). James wants to make sure we remember.

Mercy greets the homeless at the door and invites him into the presence of God's family. Mercy embraces the widow that is so lonely she can hardly breathe. Mercy supplies the fatherless with a family of faith and the necessities of life. Mercy sees beyond the wealth of a person to understand her worries and concerns. Mercy uses her freedom to spread grace without pride or prejudice. Mercy triumphs over judgment. 3:16

---

[1]Mike Yankoski, *Under the Overpass: A Journey of Faith on the Streets of America* (Sisters, OR: Multnomah, 2005).

✝

C
H
A
P
T
E
R

3   *Playing Favorites*

Rising to Perfection

1. What people do you encounter that cause you to prejudge them? Be sure to include people that you judge negatively (you think less of them automatically) and those you judge positively (you tend to assume they are just fine).

2. When we talk about religion and worship, why are we more likely to think of a "worship service" before we think of an "act of service"?

3. What kind of people would walk into your church and feel welcome and wanted automatically? Why? What about the culture of your church would attract one type of person over another? What barriers (intentional or unintentional) do you see making some feel less than welcome?

4. Treating people with mercy and consistently treating people like Jesus would transform most churches. However, it's more complex than simply saying, "We treat poor people the same as we treat rich people." Some churches treat people with equal apathy. For you as a Christian, what would it mean personally to treat people the way Jesus treats you? What specific changes would you need to make?

5. Certain situations can bring the worst out in all of us when it comes to judgmental attitudes. When have you noticed a personal tendency towards judgment instead of a tendency towards mercy?

Memory Verse
James 1:27

Religion that God our Father accepts as pure and faultless is this: to look after orphans and widows in their distress and to keep oneself from being polluted by the world.

CHAPTER FOUR

GOOD FOR
NOTHING

JAMES 2:14-26

G ood for nothing." Don't you hate the sound of that? It seems so negative. It seems so definitive. It seems very harsh and extreme. But, perhaps we need to hear it sometimes.

We drive a lot in California. Our home is positioned halfway between San Francisco and Lake Tahoe. No matter which direction I drive, the landscape changes except for one feature: thousands of cars. On our last trip to Tahoe we saw a car that made us laugh. We call them "box cars" because they literally look like a box with wheels. Apparently they are popular overseas and are making strides in the U.S.

Most of our friends who have "box cars" defend them like they were their own children or their favorite pet. One motorist that day didn't. He had a bumper sticker with a clear message:

Which means? Good for nothing. Just a pile of junk! It was one way for a customer to fight back against a sour deal that wasn't working out for him.

When we are upset about how something is or isn't working out, we tend to get a little—or a lot—negative. If our kids are making decisions that ruin their lives, we have to speak up, and sometimes it gets direct and a little ugly. When God has been frustrated with his children—well, you get the idea.

James 2:14-26 is a passage like this. We read his words with an emphasis on the negative. I believe we also should look at the positive. I decided it would be good to do both and devote two very different chapters to the same passage. This chapter is going to start with the overarching message that James is trying to convey: Christians who claim faith but don't act on their faith are fooling themselves.

Christians who don't act on their faith are fooling themselves.

In order for James to have that "fair hearing" we want him to have, let's just read his word as written:

> Do not merely listen to the word, and so deceive yourselves. Do what it says. Anyone who listens to the word but does not do what it says is like a man who looks at his face in a mirror and, after looking at himself, goes away and immediately forgets what he looks like. But the man who looks intently into the perfect law that gives freedom, and continues to do this, not forgetting what he has heard, but doing it—he will be blessed in what he does (1:22-25).
>
> What good is it, my brothers, if a man claims to have faith but has no deeds? Can such faith save him? Suppose a brother or sister is without clothes and daily food. If one of you says to him, "Go, I wish you well; keep warm and well fed," but does nothing about his physical needs, what good is it? In the same way, faith by itself, if it is not accompanied by action, is dead.
>
> But someone will say, "You have faith; I have deeds."
>
> Show me your faith without deeds, and I will show you my faith by what I do. You believe that there is one God. Good! Even the demons believe that—and shudder.
>
> You foolish man, do you want evidence that faith without deeds is useless? Was not our ancestor Abraham considered righteous for what he did when he offered his son Isaac on the altar? You see that his faith and his actions were working together, and his faith was made complete by what he did. And the scripture was fulfilled that says, "Abraham believed God, and it was credited to him as righteousness," and he was called God's friend. You see that a person is justified by what he does and not by faith alone.
>
> In the same way, was not even Rahab the prostitute considered righteous for what she did when she gave lodging to the spies and sent them off in a different direction? As the body without the spirit is dead, so faith without deeds is dead (2:14-26).

First, we have to acknowledge some reasonable assumptions based on James's words. The Christians he's writing to must have fallen into the enticing life of sitting and listening. You know the kind of existence, "If I learn something, I feel like I've really been to church!" A corrective message from James might sound somewhat different, "If I do something based on what I learned, I really feel like I am the church."

Second, we have to hear the direct message of James: Faith that doesn't act is absolutely good for nothing. It has no purpose. It has no life. It is, in a word, DEAD. Given the current state of the American church setting, this can't be read without feeling like James wrote this 2,000 years ago just for our benefit. It's not that we have the cart before the horse. Our cart and horse aren't even hooked up. They're on completely different roads. We've got the cart right with us, but we dismissed the horse and are content studying the cart!

> We've dismissed the horse and are content studying the cart.

Now before you stop reading this chapter, let me assure you we're going to flip this coin in the next study. But this side of the coin is similar to the prophetic voices of old, and it's worth taking a closer look. After all, how enjoyable do you think the message of God through Amos sounded when he first spoke these words?

> I hate, I despise your religious feasts; I cannot stand your assemblies. Even though you bring me burnt offerings and grain offerings, I will not accept them. Though you bring choice fellowship offerings, I will have no regard for them. Away with the noise of your songs! I will not listen to the music of your harps (Amos 5:21-23).

And yet, these words are some of the most powerfully shaping words in Scripture and are probably due for resurgence in the American worship setting. So are the words of James.

We commend Christian intellect and give it priority over action while God notices people who act despite their intellectual prowess. Examples of this include Cornelius in Acts because of his active prayer life and his charitable contributions to the local synagogue. Or take the widow who put the two mites into the coffers as she entered into the temple. She's not known for her intellect but for her sacrifice. We have no indication that Lazarus was a brilliant beggar. All we know is that he was cast aside by man and embraced by God.

However, I know from the inside that churches interview potential ministers based primarily on their college degrees more than on their activity of their faith. I know that we can make a great case that people need to understand why they do what they do before they do it. But James is making an equally valid point that something needs to be done in order for faith to be considered living faith.

One of my favorite children's movies is the original *Jungle Book*. The entire conversation between the buzzards is an example of many churches.

"What do you want to do?"

"I don't know."

"Well, let's do something!"

"Okay, what do you want to do?"

"I don't know. . . ."

I'd say, "No offense," but I'm honestly not sure that James is worried about offending as much as he is concerned with stirring people of faith into action. Let's be honest here, many pews are filled with sedentary members who are in the maintenance business.

I work with a guy named Larry Stafford who is a living demonstration of why churches should reconsider expanding their models and assumptions about degrees and discipleship. In the '80s Larry was riding a motorcycle with the Hell's Angels and devoting his life to the pursuit of pleasure. In the early '90s he came face-to-face with the consequences of a destructive lifestyle and decided to seek God by visiting every church on "church-row."

His search for God landed him at the Cordova Church of Christ and brought him into relationship with an elder of the church who was willing to help him save his marriage and family. Not only was the marriage saved, but he was saved in the process. Less than five years later, Larry was brought onto staff full-time as an evangelist/outreach minister. He had never attended a Christian college or received an accredited degree. But his salvation sent him on a journey for knowledge that was to be paired with his knowledge gained through the University of Life and Hard Knocks.

Larry never developed a love of sitting and listening. He developed a love of learning and acting. His frustration is the frustration of Christians everywhere: we have the greatest message ever, so let's do something because of it and with it.

James writes a scathing review of faith without works. How do you even demonstrate faith without works? There's only one way I can think of, and it is similar to the scene Paul walks into at the Areopagus. The description by Luke is simple and to the point: "All the Athenians and the foreigners who lived there spent their time doing nothing but talking about and listening to the latest ideas" (Acts 17:21). This is a style of faith that many have bought into. It has to do with debating and discussing and arguing and thinking and questioning but never acting.

What made Mother Teresa's worldwide impact so profound was her simple act of faith serving people one at a time. No one needed an

Good for Nothing

SAT or IQ test to wonder if her ministry was valid. No one needed to see her credentials to validate her faith. This kind of story is played out across the worldwide mission field. One example of this is the Ethiopian mission work being carried out by Brother Behailu Abebe. The mission started when the Ethiopian missionaries were required by the Ethiopian government to begin a social program that would benefit the nation. Without a social program, they weren't allowed to stay in Ethiopia. After studying the needs in the country, they chose to start deaf schools in order to gain permission to continue. Through the next two decades the deaf schools increased and the work began to grow. However, in the 1980s the mission to Ethiopia expanded greatly when Ethiopia suffered the drought and famine that caught the world's attention. Churches of Christ stepped forward and offered the highest level of contributions to help ease the suffering. The Ethiopian mission has now turned to teaching communities how to install drip irrigation farms and drilling wells that provide the first consistent source of well water. As of 2007 they had drilled enough wells to provide water for 900,000 Ethiopians according to UNICEF estimates. While the growth was steady during the first two decades, it's no mistake that the incredible needs of the 1980s opened the door for incredible growth.

What can we learn from these examples? Simply this: When the church desires to (or is required to), it can engage in meaningful acts of ministry that demonstrate faith to the community and to the world. It also inspires the Christians who are close enough or involved enough with the work to witness what God is doing. Faith in action is inspiring to everyone because it is authentic.

> Faith in action is inspiring to everyone because it is authentic.

People know what they see when they look at the church. Right now they don't see what they need to see in America. One of the best comments by the character Forrest Gump is, "I'm not a smart man, but I know what love is."[1] People who aren't intellectually oriented can see faith when it's made complete by action. They may not be smart, but they know authentic faith when they see it. When they see faith without action they don't see faith at all; they see modern religion that's good for nothing. Faith that's empty.

Empty faith, according to James, leaves people empty as well. It leaves people who have needs empty handed with nothing but a nice pat on the back. Churches have become their own worst enemies in this area. When I used to work as a youth minister, we faced practical concerns when we took the kids on the road. We traveled to Washington state each summer for camp and Ensenada, Mexico, for service.

After one trip to Mexico, we broke down on the road. Surprisingly we ended up just a block from a local church. It was Sunday evening and the neighborhood wasn't the best. It was getting dark and my mind started working overtime considering all the bad things that could happen having 40 tired teenagers hanging out in a public park.

We made a call to the pastor of the local church. His response? "It takes too long to turn off the alarm system to let you in." Imagine that: The church is so concerned protecting its possessions it can't help protect God's people. Unfortunately, I don't think this is uncommon. How many of us have become so jaded by the lies of junkies and con artists that we have bought into the habit of patting people on the back and wishing them well without taking care of their immediate needs?

Our church policy is this: Anyone desperate enough to beg for food at least can be given something to eat. We don't want anyone going hungry. We can help with public transportation too since the bus stop is literally in front of our campus. Many American churches are more than comfortable with schools, farms, and social outreach ministries in foreign countries but are hesitant when it comes to our own backyards. We then sit back and wonder why growth in foreign mission fields is booming and the Christian population in America is declining.

There is good news when it comes to James's indictment of churches and Christians who don't demonstrate faith through action: The younger generation is getting it. Books like *Blue like Jazz* by Donald Miller and *Under the Overpass* are being circulated through the younger generations and igniting their desire to make a difference in the world here and abroad. Many who are influenced by these concepts have given up on established congregations consumed with "doing church" and maintaining the status quo and have moved to newly planted churches that are determined to make social action a higher priority. The problem is that this often leaves local churches without the young, vibrant faith that can sustain growth for years to come. These young thinkers have arrived at a fork in the road and are deciding that faith has to do something.

These kinds of thoughts are what leave so many reading James with a hangover from guilt. Guilt isn't James's goal; guilt comes as a consequence of inactive faith. Faith is his goal. Walking around guilty because you're not doing enough is really a disease that can be avoided by simply letting your faith out of the bag, finding some fresh air, and allowing your faith to live.

> Guilt isn't James's goal, but it's a consequence of inactive faith.

James has the boldness to lay it on the line and simply say that faith without works isn't faith at all. It's dead. It's just head knowledge. And that's saying it softly. James's final statement is actually very sobering and morbid. He refers to a body without a spirit—he's talking about either a comatose existence (at best) or a corpse (most likely). Either state is undesirable. The first has the hope of waking up. Churches in this state have people surrounding them hoping they'll awaken and live one day.

Many churches are not even comatose; they're dying on the vine or have already passed on. Their members have come to the conclusion that the corpse can't be revived—no life is left. Churches like this are closing their doors or voting themselves out of existence. They are dead years before they realize it and sadly leave people in the community with a bad taste in their mouth about the lack of lived faith.

Active faith is necessary to revive these kinds of churches. Sadly, this is what they resist. Active faith isn't content with sedentary existence. It isn't compatible with tradition that ties the hands of the faithful. It demands that if Jesus did it or taught it, we should do it. It demands that if something is biblically endorsed, that the people of God be allowed to put it into practice. Active faith is creative because it is born from a God that we call our "Creator."

Suggestion

The trap of becoming sedentary, inactive Christian churches can and must be prevented. It may be a good idea for us to pretend we live in Ethiopia under the government's rule: if you're a church you have to first prove you serve the community, meaning you have to start a meaningful mission or ministry. This would revolutionize most American churches and radically change their entire structure. Most of our churches are designed to serve believers rather than equip believers to serve the community, which is our true purpose. 3:16

---

[1]*Forrest Gump* directed by Robert Zemeckis; produced by Wendy Finerman, Steve Tisch, Steve Starkey; screenplay by Eric Roth (United States: Paramount Pictures, 1994).

Rising to Perfection

1. Make a list from this study that describes useless faith—faith that's good for nothing.

    a.

    b.

    c.

    d.

    e.

2. Discuss this concept: Applied knowledge at the right place and time is wisdom. A wise person is able to apply the knowledge he has in an appropriate way. When we know a great deal about Christ but don't apply it, in what ways does that make us fools?

3. No one sets out to have useless faith. How do we lull ourselves into an existence of spiritual sleep? What contributes to the problem?

4. When are you tempted to become primarily a hearer rather than a "doer"?

5. Brainstorm 10 ideas with your friends for moving to a balance of hearing and acting at the church where you attend. Be specific, realistic, and practical with your ideas. Pray over the list and commit to moving forward with one of your action items.

 Memory Verse James 2:26

As the body without the spirit is dead, so faith without deeds is dead.

‡

C
H
A
P
T
E
R

Good for Nothing 4

CHAPTER FIVE

GOOD FOR SOMETHING

JAMES 2:14-26

T hree words that we hate when we're kids: "Don't do that!" No matter what we're doing and how harmful it might be, we wouldn't be doing it if we didn't want to be doing it. So when someone says, "Don't do that!" it infringes on our freedom.

One of the reasons James sometimes gets a bad reputation is because people read his words negatively. In our last chapter we looked at the second half of chapter two from a negative aspect. We considered faith that is good for nothing. We almost exclusively consider James 2:14-26 as negative rather than positive. In this chapter, we want to reverse that and look at the positive side.

Here's what I mean. If your parents tell you not to run into the street, it sounds negative, but the result is positive. Our lives are protected by obedience to this rule. When James says, "Faith without works is dead," we would be wise to consider the flip side of the coin and make sure we digest the positive statement he is making. If we did this, here's how his words might sound:

> It's good, my fellow believers, when you claim to have faith and back it up with works that imitate the good works of Jesus. This kind of faith can save you. Suppose a person is without clothes and food. When one of you says, "Go, I wish you well; keep warm and well fed," and back it up with the money and provision to take care of his physical needs, you're being like Christ and that's a good thing. Faith, when it's accompanied by action, is alive and vibrant!
>
> But someone will say, "You have faith; I have deeds." You can tell

me about your faith, but it's even better when you can show me faith by what you do—and that's what I see you doing!

Some people believe in one God and that's good. But we need to remember that the demons have no doubt that God exists. The difference is that their actions oppose faith in God and your actions show that you are God's. This is the kind of faith that our ancestor Abraham had. He was considered righteous for what he did when he offered his son Isaac on the altar. You see that his faith and his actions were working together, and his faith was made complete by what he did. It demonstrated that he was wholly given to God—he had vibrant faith. And the scripture was fulfilled that says, "Abraham believed God, and it was credited to him as righteousness," and he was called God's friend.

We are friends of God when our actions and faith work together to complete one another. Sometimes we believe, but our belief needs action to support it. Sometimes we are going through the motions but need our belief to give purpose to our Christian works. These two go hand in hand. You see that a person is justified by what he does when it is completing what he believes.

In the same way, was not even Rahab the prostitute considered righteous for what she did when she gave lodging to the spies and sent them off in a different direction? When our mortal bodies have a soul, they are alive. In the same way when our faith has actions, it is alive and well (2:14-26, alterations mine).

Think about this: If a person has faith but no works, that faith is good for nothing. But if a person has faith *and* works, that faith is good for something, if not good for everything! I know that much of the New Testament is written to correct bad behavior because we often need correction and discipline. Let's also keep in mind, though, God believes in rewarding those *who through their faith and life* are seeking Him (see Heb 11:6). It's worthy of a second look through these "rose-colored glasses."

> If a person has both faith and works, that faith is good for a lot!

A parallel passage in James that needs to be considered here is James 1:22-25:

> Do not merely listen to the word, and so deceive yourselves. Do what it says. Anyone who listens to the word but does not do what it says is like a man who looks at his face in a mirror and, after looking at himself, goes away and immediately forgets what he looks like. But the man who looks intently into the perfect law that gives freedom, and continues to do this, not forgetting what he has heard, but doing it—*he will be blessed in what he does* (emphasis mine).

Right off the bat we need to pay attention to the reasoning of James for Christian action. Again, it has to do with our spiritual well-being. "He will be blessed in what he does" literally means, "You will be well-off because of what you do." The translators don't take this approach to avoid a health and wealth gospel message: "If you're living a godly life, God will make you physically healthy and wealthy."

We use the term "well-off" to indicate material wealth or physical health. However, a person could be "well-off" while being physically sick and spiritually healthy. While I was growing up, one of my role models exemplified this lifestyle. His name was Billy Searcy.

Billy was a regular face in our worship services. He was a quadriplegic who never missed a Sunday except for surgical procedures or sickness. In a tragic accident shortly after his wedding, Billy was destined for a limited existence for the rest of his adult life. His faithful wife, Sharon, brought him to church every week until Billy died several years ago.

As a young boy, I loved it when Billy was asked to lead the prayer at church. The microphone was delivered to Billy. He always sat just behind and to the left of the youth ministry. This meant he was located close to the front where he could see and participate. While you could barely make out the words, you could always understand the heart.

Our preachers often spoke about evangelism and knocking on doors. They often called on the church to get the message out by taking time to walk the neighborhoods. Billy couldn't walk so he found another opportunity: lying in traction for months while his surgical wounds healed. It was in those weeks of pain and suffering that he did his best evangelistic work.

Billy's body was shattered while his soul was running a marathon. I'm not going to sit here and pretend that Billy's physical condition didn't affect his attitude and spirituality in ways that we probably didn't see. What I can tell you is that his faithful struggle and Sharon's faithful love made a difference in the lives of every person who witnessed their walk with God and each other. His works of prayer and evangelism coupled with Sharon's work of love and perseverance made for a complete, whole Christian life.

Actions complete faith. I also believe the opposite is true: faith completes action. You can believe God intellectually, but when you couple that belief with action, it becomes living faith, *vibrant faith*. This is the kind of faith that makes a difference. It's the faith that takes Abraham to the top of the mountain while his heart is breaking

> When you couple intellectual belief with action it becomes vibrant faith.

with anguish. It's the faith that helps Enoch wake up every day and walk with God. It's the faith that builds an ark in a dry desert, steps into a lion's den in prayer, stands in a fiery furnace untouched, believes that every disaster and blessing in life was brought about by the will of God for the saving of Egypt and the sons of Israel, and on and on we could go if this were a study of Hebrews 11 and not a study of James.

God commends people of faith, not people of intellectual belief. God notices and God commends. You're doing it right when you allow your faith to take you places. You're doing it right when you take that scary step of faith and allow God to lead you. You're doing it right when you cross the comfort zone into the service zone. It may feel weird and sometimes manufactured, but practice makes perfect.

> Living in the "service zone" may feel weird at first, but practice makes perfect.

For years, coaching soccer was a highlight of my life. A former member of the German National Team brought a group of children to a VBS program I was running, and he immediately approached me with an idea: He knew soccer, and I knew kids. If we put his knowledge together with my communication skills, we could have great success. We coached together for two years in Ft. Worth, Texas.

Our team was ranked so low based on mathematical formulas that we had to be moved up two divisions just to be in a bracket with other teams. In other words, no other teams scored low enough to be division four or five—without our team, division three was the lowest division of any team. Just like faith is completed by works, his knowledge completed my words. In the end, it took a top select team with paid coaches to eliminate our ragtag bunch of boys in the championship game.

When our boys first met, most of them were just like their new coach: never played soccer, and didn't know anything about it. We practiced together every evening we could. We practiced until even the coaching staff was getting in shape. We eventually played in games and did well, but first we had to practice.

Just like practice makes perfect in sports, it works in church as well. Too often churches devote all of their time studying the game and never practicing. Healthy churches usually have three components of Christian action: study, practice, and playing. When you study all the time, you run short on time to practice what you've just learned. When you practice all the time, you live without understanding, but you also miss the component of taking your actions into a world of disbelief. When you combine all three . . . well, you end up with vibrant faith.

When I was preaching on James, a thought occurred to me: if I would preach like I coach soccer, it might make a difference in the way people put their faith into action. On each of the teams I coached, every practice had mistakes. However, every practice had moments of absolutely beautiful execution that needed to be celebrated. Yeah, I'd yell corrective instructions to the kids when they missed their assignment. However, nothing got more vocal and physical reaction than a play well practiced. Our coaching staff would go nuts to the point that the boys and parents would laugh in disbelief.

What happened as a result was amazing . . . and predictable. The team would repeat what they had just done over and over in order to get the same result from the coaches. I had noticed coaches that were like many preachers—yell at the mistakes and ignore the successes and always leave the team feeling they should've and could've done better.

During the summer I was working on this text, it dawned on me that my local congregation was preparing to send the fourth and fifth teams to help de-muck homes that were destroyed by hurricane Katrina. An additional team was preparing to leave for Japan. In the fall another team helping with medical missions in Guatemala would represent us in that work. All of this was in addition to our local community camp offered free-of-charge to the area children. People were hearing the words of James and deciding to implement what they were hearing. People of faith were letting their faith breathe and have life, and God, I'm sure, was taking notice.

> People of faith were letting their faith have life, and God was taking notice.

God is our Father and what parent doesn't smile when his child demonstrates an ability to use what he's learned? As a minister, I've been energized by the stories of those who have engaged in active, missional faith. In my mind, I imagine God not only energized, but standing on the sidelines screaming with great enthusiasm, "I knew you could do it!" I believe God is excited every time his children embrace saving faith instead of observational faith.

We need to keep in mind that there is a considerable difference between saving faith and salvation by works. James has been misunderstood on this point. We are considered innocent and free when we put our faith into action. James uses the term "freedom" in 1:25 and the term "justified" in 2:24 to describe the person who combines faith with Christian action. We understand freedom, but justification is more difficult. It literally can be interpreted "rendered innocent." Forgiven is one thing; declared to be innocent is another. God can look at us and see our childlike innocence when we put feet under our faith.

We all have a long list of shortcomings. But let's remember that God's book is a book of life filled with the names of his innocent children—children made innocent by the blood of the Lamb (see Rev 21:27). God appreciates effort on the part of his children like any parent appreciates effort. He disapproves of laziness as any parent disapproves of laziness. Our faith needs to live and breathe.

James is not only saying, "Faith without works is dead." He's also saying, "Faith with works is alive!"

Taking the Step of Faith

James compares and contrasts two kinds of common faith: one that is consumed with listening and learning and another based on hearing and doing. Modern churches consume the clock by sitting, listening, and being impressed with increased knowledge (or technologically advanced worship). We shouldn't be surprised that this isn't appealing to the younger generations. They're impressed when someone actually takes the word to heart and puts it into action. If it's not put into action, they wonder if it actually got into the heart.

Postmodern worship services throw the sit-and-listen generations off. Instead of imagining the anointing of oil, they actually anoint people with oil. They lift hands instead of giving it lip service. They partake in communion instead of passing communion. Whatever is passive, they dismiss, and whatever is active, they embrace. It's making a loud statement without articulating a single word: we need to see faith and feel faith.

God is impressed by wisdom—the application in life of what we know. I'd suggest that James is calling for the people of God to ask for and demonstrate wisdom. Put what you know into practice. There's a phrase I picked up at some seminar somewhere (I can't remember when or where, but I like it): "The church doesn't need more members; it needs more disciples." When you say this, the passive pew people get upset and the active, "let's put it into action" people get fired up.

> "The church doesn't need more members; it needs more disciples."

Jesus taught by words and deeds. He educated, demonstrated, encouraged, and expected action. He taught his disciples by having them sit and listen. He demonstrated what he meant by showing them examples from everyday life with everyday people. He encouraged them by trusting them to go out into the community and demonstrate by doing. He expected them to continue this process after he ascended into heaven.

Casting Crowns wrote a song entitled "If We Are the Body" that reinforces James's message. The chorus of this song prods us to act out

47

‡

C
H
A
P
T
E
R

our faith. It asks, "If we are the Body, why aren't we out in the world using our arms and hands and legs and mouths to reach, heal, teach, go, and show people the way?" We are his body. We are reaching. We are healing. We are teaching. We are going. We are showing that Jesus is the way. But we can improve and we can do more. Not because we feel guilty but because we embrace the freedom we've been given through the loving act of Jesus Christ.

How do works lead to salvation without our salvation being based on works? Try this out: Jesus went to the cross, and because of his action we have salvation. I don't think anyone would suggest that that's bad theology.

What most of us need is a reorientation towards discipleship or a stronger orientation towards discipleship. Most of us are degree-oriented. Our society believes if a person has a degree, he is qualified. We assume that academics will lead to action. The problem is we all know PhD's who are incompetent. Discipleship orientation is different from degree orientation. When we are discipleship-oriented, we allow people to function like apprentices—someone who learns on the job. When apprentices have completed their training, they know what they're doing. Jesus sought action not academics. If we are disciples, we have enrolled in an apprenticeship for life. We learn through education, demonstration, encouragement, and expectation. We must possess a faith that acts, not just a faith that knows. This kind of faith is good for something!! 3:16

Rising to Perfection

1. Consider people you know who have put their faith into action. Tell a story about this kind of faith. What did it look like? What impact did it have on you and the people who witnessed this life?

2. Every Christian can look back and see moments when their faith and actions made a difference Without bragging about it, it's okay to talk about it for the edification of others. When has this kind of faith been exhibited in your life?

3. What tempts you to conform to sitting and listening faith? Why is intellectual belief appealing to people?

4. Think about this statement: "It's not what you know. It's not who you know. It's not what you do. It's what you do because of what you know that makes for biblical faith." Would you agree with that statement?

5. Why is it important not only to balance faith and works, but to keep them tied together? In what ways are they absolutely inseparable?

Memory Verse
James 2:24

You see that a person is justified by what he does when it is completing what he believes (paraphrased).

CHAPTER SIX

A POWERFUL PALATE

JAMES 3:1-12

When I was at Abilene Christian University, one of my best friends invited me to visit his family in Dallas. I had a great weekend enjoying the hospitality of his family. I honestly can't remember any detail about the weekend other than the nickname his mom gave me: The Mouth. It was then I began to realize a truth of life: every person's greatest strength is also their greatest weakness.

I'm a perfect example of this. My mouth is what I use to preach. Vocal communication is the tool God has given me to use for his glory. Vocal communication is also my greatest weakness. It's my ability to talk that also results in a serious case of "foot-in-mouth" disease. The same gift that allows me to think fast on my feet while teaching God's Word and professing truth is the same weakness that results in quick responses that haven't been thought out. My greatest strength is my greatest weakness.

Apparently this was a problem for other people long before I was born. James bore witness to this fact 2,000 years ago, but the truth resonates today. We use our mouths to praise God. But is it just lip service?

James writes:

> Not many of you should presume to be teachers, my brothers, because you know that we who teach will be judged more strictly. We all stumble in many ways. If anyone is never at fault in what he says, he is a perfect man, able to keep his whole body in check.

When we put bits into the mouths of horses to make them obey us, we can turn the whole animal. Or take ships as an example. Although they are so large and are driven by strong winds, they are steered by a very small rudder wherever the pilot wants to go. Likewise the tongue is a small part of the body, but it makes great boasts. Consider what a great forest is set on fire by a small spark. The tongue also is a fire, a world of evil among the parts of the body. It corrupts the whole person, sets the whole course of his life on fire, and is itself set on fire by hell.

All kinds of animals, birds, reptiles and creatures of the sea are being tamed and have been tamed by man, but no man can tame the tongue. It is a restless evil, full of deadly poison.

With the tongue we praise our Lord and Father, and with it we curse men, who have been made in God's likeness. Out of the same mouth come praise and cursing. My brothers, this should not be. Can both fresh water and salt water flow from the same spring? My brothers, can a fig tree bear olives, or a grapevine bear figs? Neither can a salt spring produce fresh water (3:1-12).

This discussion begins with a peculiar word of advice from James— let's not have too many teachers! When was the last time you heard that in a church? As a matter of fact, most congregations of believers are constantly begging for new teachers. "Every one of you should take a turn teaching." At face value it would seem that James is saying exactly the opposite,

We miss the point here because what we term "teacher" and what James referred to as "teacher" are two different things. James speaks about those who are "master teachers." Some like to use the term "teacher of teachers" to describe the concept. This term doesn't describe those who would like to step into the nursery class. Imagine, "If you help teach babies, you'll be subject to a greater judgment." This wouldn't make any sense.

However, those of us who teach those who teach—those who shape the theology and thinking of the church— need to approach the opportunity with great care. Why? Because words shape people. Words change lives! Relatively few people would recognize Martin Luther King, Jr., if he was walking down the street in regular street clothes. On the other hand, most anyone could simply hear the words, "I have a dream," and recognize one of the greatest figures known to American culture and freedom.

Words are powerful. With them we can rule kingdoms, destroy peace, reconcile differences, and build or destroy faith. James uses several analogies to help us understand how powerful the mouth is. It's

Words shape people. Words change lives.

like a bit in a horse's mouth, a rudder on a ship, or a spark in a dry forest.

I grew up in the country and had the occasional opportunity to ride horses. Allegra was the horse I rode most often. She was a powerful horse with more than a little spirit. If you knew what you were doing, you could lead this horse anywhere you wanted to go. The operative word is "if."

One year I was invited to be Allegra's first rider after she had given birth to a new colt. We headed to the end of the property with Allegra fighting us all the way. She only wanted one thing: to be with her baby. When we gave up and turned back toward the barn, Allegra agreed with our decision. As a matter of fact, she was very eager and took off.

It was at this point that I realized my inability to control her. She bolted for home and I held on for dear life. The friend riding next to me was a more accomplished rider. She pulled up alongside and grabbed the reins and with just a few maneuvers was able to stop disaster and control Allegra's return back to the stable and her colt. With just two straps of leather and a piece of metal, this power was contained.

The largest warship is controlled by one person who operates the rudder. In the same way the direction of a relationship can be turned with one word. I'm not saying it should be this way . . . it just is. One right word can make all the difference in the world, while one wrong word can close the door of friendship forever.

For those of us living in California, James's analogy of a spark and fire is sadly too close for comfort. I moved to the Golden State during November when the hills are lush with florescent green grass. From November to April the rain makes the Golden State more like the Garden State. Then the rain stops and the golden brown monopolizes the state until the cycle of winter returns.

Every year it only takes one flat tire to spark a fire. One cigarette butt thrown in the wrong place, and the entire state goes up in smoke. One mistake making s'mores and a family memory turns into a nightmare. This is true with words. Words cause wars. Words shape politics. Words reveal who we really are and what we really want.

This is such a central teaching of James that he makes a bold claim: "If anyone is never at fault in what he says, he is a perfect man, able to keep his whole body in check." We know a person can't be perfect. We know none of us can keep our whole body in check. James is making a very bold claim: no one is perfect when it comes to words.

> No one is perfect when it comes to words.

We try. We hire speech writers for the President. We screen comments for every statement made by the Federal Chairman. We have scripts for actors, scripts for politicians, scripts for preachers, scripts for teachers. We write these scripts so the right words will be said by the right people at the right time. Then an amazing thing happens . . . the President answers a question, the chairman speaks out of turn, an actor goes on a talk show, or a teacher strays from the textbook.

In 2006 Hollywood was treated to a crash course in words gone astray. The wildly successful movie series *Mission Impossible* was entering its third production in as many years. The star of the show, Tom Cruise, took to the talk-show circuit to promote the movie. The problem was that he strayed from the script and began promoting his new wife and theology of childbirth based on beliefs from Scientology. When he vocalized his beliefs about women keeping quiet during the birthing process, the women responded. They responded with unusual silence during the talk shows and in turn spoke loudly by refusing to pay to see the movie.

What was supposed to be a blockbuster May release ended up being a late spring dud. Damage control couldn't convince the public to attend. Getting Cruise back on script during promotional shows didn't help. Even positive critiques in the national media couldn't get people back. Bragging about his wife's silence during the birthing process only made things worse. The rest of the year the movie moved down the money list for one reason: he opened his mouth and allowed us to look into his heart. The truth is that most actors are viewed favorably because they always have their words carefully crafted *for them*. They usually speak from a script—something no one can do 100% of the time.

Words, according to Jesus, do something we need to pay attention to: they reveal who we are from the inside out. "The good man brings good things out of the good stored up in his heart, and the evil man brings evil things out of the evil stored up in his heart. For out of the overflow of his heart his mouth speaks" (Luke 6:45). Words originate in our hearts and deep within our heads. Once they come out of the mouth, these internal thoughts are revealed.

Words reveal who we are from the inside out.

People say that extemporaneous speaking is "speaking off the top of your head." Actually it's speaking off the top of our heads *and hearts*. If we could control our heads and hearts, we could control our mouths. We can't and so we won't! We will make mistakes with our words. Because of that, not many of us should sign up for shaping faith through teaching (and preaching for that matter).

Being a preacher I hear fun little jabs taken at public speakers. "It's not like it's a big deal; it was just a sermon. People forget what you say before they walk out the door." Glad to say that's not true; sad to say that's not true. I'm pleased that good words have an impact, and I'm embarrassed that bad words often have a greater impact.

Although James makes these comments in the context of master teachers, the instructions about controlling the tongue are meant for everyone. We should be consistent in our praise of God and encouragement of his creation. Paul says in 2 Corinthians 10:8 that he would, ". . . boast somewhat freely about the authority the Lord gave [him] for building [the believers] up rather than pulling you down." Paul is talking about doing this with words.

We defend our rights in America, but how often do you hear someone defending their right to build people up and not tear them down? On the contrary, we reserve the right to run people down whenever we like. We use words to do this. Sometimes it's dramatic and makes the front page headlines. Other times it's private and comes in a whisper. The effects are the same: the same mouth we use to elevate God is used to humiliate his creation he loves.

You may not be aware of this, but there is a "bird world" that exists in America. We walked into this world when be bought Peaches—our first and last bird, a Cockatoo. What I didn't know is that birds can be trained to go to the bathroom on command. It's a long process, but to keep it short for our purposes here, you can actually train a bird to go to the bathroom on the count of three, giving you 15-17 minutes of accident free roaming around the house or yard.

Isn't it strange that we can potty-train a bird, house-train a dog, train a mouse, train a rat (of all things), but can't control our own mouths? Words barely leave our mouths and we're reaching out with both hands to pull them back in . . . but, too late, they're out there and they will be heard.

> Isn't it strange that we can potty-train a bird but can't control our own mouths?

James is calling us to maturity, driving us toward perfection. He wants us to at least try the impossible, at least show some effort. Let that final fruit of the spirit—self-control—have a chance to flourish in our mouths. Otherwise, it's a shocking sadness when our words destroy our discipleship.

I'll never forget my first experience in the Caribbean. The water looked like it had been dyed the perfect hue of blue and green. I had seen pictures, but nothing captured the beauty of it. The problem with the beautiful Caribbean is that no matter how clear it looks, it's still saltwater. All it takes is one splash in the eyes to realize it may look clear and refreshing, but it's not fresh water.

You can only drink fresh water and quench your thirst; you can only hear encouraging words and leave edified. You can only get grapes from a vine and figs from a tree; you should only get godly language from God's people.

This call by James for an overhaul on our speech is a call for vocal perfection that he knows we can't and won't attain—but we should give a shot. Why? If we know we're going to fall short, why try? Because, effort makes a difference. If you don't try to control your tongue, it will do untold damage. God forgives our weakness with words just as he forgives our sins of sensuality. But just like disciples are called to a higher control of sexuality, we are also challenged to speak from a new script.

A New Script

God may not give us a line-by-line script on a teleprompter but he does offer us some basics that can help. First, being conscious of the problem is the beginning. Control of the tongue begins with acknowledging that the tongue can get out of hand. Second, taking responsibility for what we say is a step in the right direction.

One summer I sold books for the Southwestern Company in Oklahoma. One weekend I took a day off to attend a youth rally. The event packed the church with excited teens devoted to God. After the event concluded, the local students who had worked hard gathered in the auditorium to enjoy some of the victories. I listened from a distance knowing how excited they must have been; their hard work had paid off.

A woman walked in the auditorium at that time and began speaking rudely to them about cleaning up the place. She ranted and raved about the paper, notes, dirt . . . just about everything. In just a few moments, she had stolen all victory from the teens and replaced victory with bitterness. No celebration was allowed; cleaning and complaining was the priority.

My face must have revealed my disapproval because one of the adults in the auditorium made a statement I've grown to hate, "Don't mind her, that's just the way she is." Not true. The good news about life is that we are how we choose to be. The good news of Jesus is that we can become who we follow; that's what discipleship is all about. This can't start, however, until we take responsibility for our right to choose. Victor Frankl, the Holocaust survivor turned author of the psychological school of thought known as "reality therapy," calls choice the greatest of human freedoms. He says that this great freedom is our ability to choose our attitude regardless of our circumstances. This was the difference he noticed between those who survived the concentration camps and those who did not.[1] It's also the difference between disciples of Christ and the world that believes "we are who we are."

The last step in this is filling our hearts and minds with something so enriching that when we speak, good comes out. Notice I didn't suggest you attempt to get rid of the bad in your heart and mind. Imagine a cup filled with red water. You can pour out the red water and you'll have less red water . . . but that's still all you have. You can try another approach—put the glass under the water spout and begin filling it with pure water. As the glass has more pure water poured in, there is less room for the red water and eventually you end up with a glass of pure water.

We spend too much time trying to empty our minds of the bad stuff when all we need to do is fill our hearts with the good stuff! When we begin to do this, our words will change. How does it happen? When our hearts are overflowing with God-thoughts, our mouths will be overflowing with Godlike language. This doesn't mean "church-chat." It means authentically caring, Christlike language that connects creation to Creator. Imagine your mouth providing more flavor to the world than it takes. It's a powerful palate that can truly ensure that your words reflect what God wants for every disciple, "Let your conversation be always full of grace, seasoned with salt, so that you may know how to answer everyone" (Col 4:6). [3:16]

---

[1]Viktor E. Frankl, *Man's Search for Meaning*, trans. by Ilse Lasch (Boston: Beacon Press, 2006).

✝

C
H
A
P
T
E
R

6 *A Powerful Palate*

Rising to Perfection

1. When you think of controlling your tongue, what's the most difficult challenge for you (sarcasm, vulgarity, harshness, etc.)?

2. Share one example of someone using words to build you up and change your life. What did he or she say that meant so much? How did it make a difference in your life?

3. What's the most difficult animal you've ever had to train? What was involved? How much work was involved?

4. If you were to begin taming your tongue, what would be the first steps you would need to take?

5. God wants all of his followers to have a powerful palate—one that is seasoned with grace, control, and encouragement. How would the "taste in your mouth" change (spiritually speaking) if you changed the contents of your heart?

6. How does it help to think of making this change by filling yourself up with good things rather than trying to empty yourself of bad things? Why can't we just empty ourselves of every bad memory, thought, etc.?

Memory Verse
James 3:9-10

With the tongue we praise our Lord and Father, and with it we curse men, who have been made in God's likeness. Out of the same mouth come praise and cursing. My brothers, this should not be.

CHAPTER SEVEN

PEACE, PERFECT PEACE

JAMES 3:13-18

In late 1995 I was honored to be sent on a trip to the Holy Lands by the local congregation where I preached. It was both a learning experience and a training experience: Learning by walking in the lands of the Bible and training for return trips in the future. The fact that traveling to Israel in recent years has been unsafe only highlights a comment that was made by our guide several times. His words have remained in my mind for the past 10 years, "We all want peace, but at what price?"

While he personally wanted to see peace in the Holy Lands, he wasn't willing to pay for peace by giving up all of Israel's lands or freedoms. It is possible for peace to cost too high a price for a nation or a person. This is what humbles us in our relationship with God. He was willing to pay the ultimate price in order to bring peace for us.

James writes in James 3:17-18, "But the wisdom that comes from heaven is first of all pure; then *peace-loving*, considerate, submissive, full of mercy and good fruit, impartial and sincere. *Peacemakers* who sow in *peace* raise a harvest of righteousness" (emphasis mine). We all want peace, but at what price?

The old hymn, "Peace, Perfect Peace," sounds really good, but we need to consider how it is achieved. James writes:

> Who is wise and understanding among you? Let him show it by his good life, by deeds done in the humility that comes from wisdom. But if you harbor bitter envy and selfish ambition in your hearts, do not boast

about it or deny the truth. Such 'wisdom' does not come down from heaven but is earthly, unspiritual, of the devil. For where you have envy and selfish ambition, there you find disorder and every evil practice.

But the wisdom that comes from heaven is first of all pure; then peace-loving, considerate, submissive, full of mercy and good fruit, impartial and sincere. Peacemakers who sow in peace raise a harvest of righteousness (3:13-18).

There are several things that can destroy peace. One of them is harboring ill feelings. The language used by James really digs deep into our hearts and minds. When we allow the ship of bitter envy to moor itself in our harbor, we cannot have peace. Harboring these feelings prevents peace.

> When we allow the ship of bitter envy to moor itself in our harbor, we cannot have peace.

When I spent time with my extended family recently, we had our regular "walk down memory lane" moments. Mom and Dad told stories about my childhood, and we all laughed. One particular story recounted my runaway experience when I was barely 10 years old.

Growing up with two older sisters, I have always known what persecution meant. Probably no greater challenge in life exists for a little boy than having two sisters who know more and have experienced more. It led to moments of humiliation (i.e., waking up in a gas station with curlers in your hair . . . only discovered because people were laughing). It led to moments of frustration. And, apparently, it led to moments of desperation.

I can't remember what set me off, but I knew what I was doing. Every good escape requires a stick with a knapsack attached to the end of it containing food and basic essentials. My food was prepared, wrapped, and tied, and off I went to pursue a better life without girls. My travels got me approximately 100 feet before my neighbor inquired what I was doing. As I described my situation to the neighbor, more questions surfaced, "Where are you going?" "Where will you sleep?" "How will you get from one place to another?" As you can guess, my trip ended and I went home.

Years removed, we sat around and laughed at the episode. With that memory, however, came back other memories I'd rather forget. Some are bitter memories that still cause personal pain and have shaped my self-image. The deepest one has to do with a nickname I received at a very young age, "Fatty."

It's funny to look at pictures from my childhood, because I am amazed at how "non-fat" I was. My daughter commented as she looked at my little league picture, "You weren't fat at all." Amazing that

Peace, Perfect Peace

when I stand in the mirror—regardless of the shape I'm in—I still see and hear, "Fatty." The primary person who chose this name disliked me for many or no reasons. I'm not sure which. He's long since ended up in jail and has had no voice in my life since the sixth grade . . . but the bitterness can be easily conjured up in just a few moments of thought. I've spent considerable energy and thought getting that ship to leave my harbor. But, it can return and begin to steal my peace.

Envious attitudes have the same effect. In the modern rendition of *The Count of Monte Cristo*, two friends are also two rivals: Dantes and Fernand. Dantes is a poor man's son who through courage and love has been given the position of Captain which will enable him to soon take the role of husband. The problem is that Fernand, the son of a wealthy and powerful father, wants the ship and wants the girl. He is consumed with envy.

He plots to have Dantes falsely accused, arrested, and imprisoned for life allowing him to attain both the boat and the woman. When Dantes is captured while being held at sword point by what he thought was his best friend, he asks the question, "Why?" Fernand's answer, "Because I'm not supposed to want to be you." In a word, "envy!"

James puts three things together that destroy peace: Bitterness, envy, and selfish ambition. Bitterness and envy almost always lead to selfish ambition. All three always lead to a life with no peace. How many stories in literature just like *The Count of Monte Cristo* try to remind man of a simple irony: you can have everything, but without contentment, you will never be happy.

> Bitterness and envy lead to selfish ambition and a life with no peace.

When James wrote about having a peaceful life, he knew this. Yes, we want peace, but at what price? What am I willing to pay for it? Am I willing to give up my bitter feelings? Am I willing to drive away envious thoughts and behavior? Am I really willing to set aside my selfish ambition? Or do I in some sort of bizarre way enjoy having those three feelings right in my own backyard?

Notice the often quoted words from James 4:15, ". . . 'If it is the Lord's will, we will live and do this or that.'" The most important words in this verse are, "If it is the Lord's will." We all know that "the Lord's will" is not compatible with bitterness, envy, and selfish ambition. As a matter of fact they are diabolically opposed.

Sometimes we feel that peace eludes us because we don't know what the Lord's will is. However, the Lord's will isn't that difficult when it comes to the broader understanding of life. It's not like God's will is some mystical, unknown, unrevealed secret unavailable to his followers. Instead it has been made known, revealed through Jesus and available through his word. Mystery will still always surround God, and by "mystery" I mean that we will never have God "figured out." But his will for daily living was intentionally made clear on most points through both the Living and written word.

The real problem is my will vs. his will. One teacher made a comment that has stayed with me through the years, "We all have to decide now what we're going to do when we disagree with God." We might claim that we agree with God, but our actions reveal that our desires are much different from God's, and our will often wins out over his will. Who can have peace when his own will is driving his life? Ask self-consumed athletes and self-promoted icons how peaceful and content their luxurious lives are. Nobody needs to ask because everybody except them can see the answer in their desperate existence.

Disciples of Christ say we desire the, "Peace that passes understanding." We write songs, "Peace like a River," and imagine in our minds the beautiful mountain stream instead of the rushing Mississippi at flood stage. And yet, attaining peace requires a price, and we have to decide if we want to pay the price.

Paying the Price for Peace

Let's think practically what this requires. James states that it begins with a life of wisdom that is backed up with humble living. Living in humility is so far removed from living in America that I'm not sure I can comprehend the changes required to attain the peace I say I want. I might make an American comment, "I'd be willing to pay anything for that kind of peace," but I fear the answer would be similar to the response to Simon in Acts 8:20, "May your money perish with you, because you thought you could buy the gift of God with money!" Paying for peace with money would be too cheap; real peace requires real payment.

The first thing we have to do in order to have this peace is let go of the life events that bring bitterness into our hearts. The wrongs done to us. The abuses by those around us. The deception of people we trusted. The betrayal of those who followed us. In other words, we have to, ". . . deny ourselves and take up our cross and follow Jesus." Bitterness is something we like because it gives us the right to gripe and complain and throw pity parties. It makes us interesting as we retell the stories of unfair treatment we have endured. In many ways bitterness becomes who we are and why we exist. You can't hold onto peace and bitterness. To hold onto one, you have to let go of the other.

You can't hold onto both peace and bitterness; you must let go of one or the other.

Holding onto bitterness is not only a temptation, it's a trend. When we talk about the stories that cause us bitterness, the conversation is usually described as friends telling "war stories." I've never been in the military and have never fired a shot in combat. And yet, people who know me have heard my war stories. It's interesting that retelling them is really reliving them. I didn't like the feelings of unrest when I experienced the events of those days, and I don't like the feelings of unrest when I re-experience them. And yet I, like many, will self-inflict the wounds by sharing the stories for no particular reason. Why? Because, like so many, I like it when bitterness makes berth in my harbor.

The second thing we have to get rid of is envy. Our lives become consumed with wanting what the other guy has. The world gives us a constant dose of, "someone else has something you don't." It's not that we need the "something else" it's just that the implication is that I have something less. We really don't live by the adage, "less is more" like we should. We live by the mantra, "more is more."

Envy, like bitterness, is a destructive quality we almost refuse to be rid of. Envy infects not only the poor in this world, but seems to also have its grip on the wealthiest in this world. Professional athletes are proof of this. In 2006 Bonzi Wells turned down a bid to play basketball for seven million dollars a year for five years not because he couldn't live off of 35 million, but because other players were being paid more and, after all, he was worth it. He ended up on the unemployment line of the NBA because of envy and greed.

We can look at players and celebrities who obviously have "envy-itis" and brag about the fact that if we had a million dollars, you'd never hear us complain. Humanity has the bad habit of seeing the speck in someone else's eye and forgetting the plank in our own eye. For me it's the desire for my kids to have the same "stuff" that other kids their age have. It's my desire to take the same kind of trips, own the same kind of phones, live in the same kind of houses that my friends all have. The truth is that even if I had all that stuff, the rest of the world would look at my kids, house, computer and say, "When I look at you, I'm not sure I see that there is a real difference."

We might do good to start envying the person who has peace and lacks material possessions. "Wow! How'd you get your hands on that kind of peace?" "Well, I had to let go of envy, and with envy went most of my material possessions that stole my peace from my life." While James doesn't make a direct comment to this effect, you sure get the impression that possessions get in the way of peace. Poverty can have

> We might do good to start "envying" the person with peace but no possessions.

the same effect, but we tend to believe if we live in the lap of luxury that peace is an automatic result of wealth. The only way to rid our lives of envy is to embrace contentment.

The third step towards peace is deciding on a new orientation in life. Instead of selfish ambition, we have to begin a pursuit of God's desires for our lives. While we can talk about this theoretically, it would be more beneficial to get right down to it and speak the truth. Without a daily devotion and walk with God, we're not going to have a daily orientation away from self. As long as our walk with God is casual and on our terms, we're not going to be walking with our cross towards the cross.

Several years ago I began to read books on the spiritual disciplines. It seemed good because the root word of disciple and discipline are one and the same. I soon discovered that very few writers from my spiritual heritage had written anything on the topic, much less a book. Why was this? My conclusion is that we've emphasized knowledge of God's word more than an intimate knowledge of God. What's the difference? One is devoted to the discussions about God while the other is in pursuit of discussions with God.

I believe our selfish ambition is completely lost when we embrace the will of God. You can't have both in your heart and mind. This is a scary thought because it brings up an uncomfortable awareness that pursuit of my own agenda guarantees I'm not pursuing his agenda. Knowing how our own agendas get us into trouble, why don't we act as true ambassadors on a mission for the King? We don't because we enjoy being the ruler of our lives and the CEO of our personal corporations. Control is an illusion. We think we can have it, but God reminds us through the events of life that control is best left in his hands.

> We think we can have control, but God reminds us that it's best left in his hands.

If you're not willing to pay God for his peace through these three currencies, you can't get your hands on the "peace that passes understanding." It's a high price because it affects everything from self-pity to self-reliance. It also requires one last thing that James mentions in this text: Wisdom and understanding. In the case of bitterness, envy, and selfish ambition wisdom has a very special role.

I don't think the abandonment of bitterness, envy, and ambition means we can't tell the "war stories" anymore. Rather, it probably means we have to let the war stories die and the wisdom stories come to life. A story that recalls hurt or suffering or abuse can be told for benefit and teaching or for self-pity and self-promotion. "Why" we tell the story dictates "how" we tell the story.

Godly people have learned how to take a story of personal suffering and use it to strengthen others rather than to condemn others, because this is exactly what God has done. His story of Jesus' death is the story of our redemption more than the story of condemnation. We need to tell these stories of redemption, hope, and peace. We can't if we have a heart filled with bitterness, envy, and selfish ambition. The peace that comes from God can only be experienced by those willing to let go of these three destructive desires. 3:18

✝

C
H
A
P
T
E
R

7   *Peace, Perfect Peace*

Rising to Perfection

1. What kind of noise disturbs your peace the most? Is it a loud stereo, blaring TV, kids being kids, etc.?

2. When you think of bitterness, what comes to mind? What kinds of experiences in life leave you with a bitter taste in your mouth?

3. "How much is enough?" is a question we all have to ask ourselves. Usually, our answer is, "A little more." In what ways can our desire for a little more make room in our hearts for envious attitudes?

4. What cultural influences make you want to pursue selfish ambitions? What is attractive about climbing over everyone on the way to the top?

5. What are three things you believe can be done to get rid of bitterness, envy, and selfish ambition? What have you seen or read that works?

| Memory Verse James 3:17-18 | *But the wisdom that comes from heaven is first of all pure; then peace-loving, considerate, submissive, full of mercy and good fruit, impartial and sincere. Peacemakers who sow in peace raise a harvest of righteousness.* |

CHAPTER EIGHT

WHAT ABOUT ME?

JAMES 4:1-17

One of the most enchanting families at church had four boys and more on the way. The youngest boy made sure you didn't forget him by asking over and over, "What about me? What about me? What about me?" While cute the first few times he did this, it quickly irritated his parents who didn't really enjoy self-oriented children. Unfortunately, they are raising kids in a self-oriented culture. American culture shouts, "It's all about me!" Our choices and decisions prove we believe it. Ultimately, it robs us of our peace.

James jumps into our American comfort zone when he challenges this notion head on. You'd think he was writing to our culture rather than his when he writes:

> What causes fights and quarrels among you? Don't they come from your desires that battle within you? You want something but don't get it. You kill and covet, but you cannot have what you want. You quarrel and fight. You do not have, because you do not ask God. When you ask, you do not receive, because you ask with wrong motives, that you may spend what you get on your pleasures.
>
> You adulterous people, don't you know that friendship with the world is hatred toward God? Anyone who chooses to be a friend of the world becomes an enemy of God. Or do you think Scripture says without reason that the spirit he caused to live in us envies intensely? But he gives us more grace. That is why Scripture says:
>
> > "God opposes the proud
> > but gives grace to the humble."

Submit yourselves, then, to God. Resist the devil, and he will flee from you. Come near to God and he will come near to you. Wash your hands, you sinners, and purify your hearts, you double-minded. Grieve, mourn and wail. Change your laughter to mourning and your joy to gloom. Humble yourselves before the Lord, and he will lift you up.

Brothers, do not slander one another. Anyone who speaks against his brother or judges him speaks against the law and judges it. When you judge the law, you are not keeping it, but sitting in judgment on it. There is only one Lawgiver and Judge, the one who is able to save and destroy. But you—who are you to judge your neighbor?

Now listen, you who say, "Today or tomorrow we will go to this or that city, spend a year there, carry on business and make money." Why, you do not even know what will happen tomorrow. What is your life? You are a mist that appears for a little while and then vanishes. Instead, you ought to say, "If it is the Lord's will, we will live and do this or that." As it is, you boast and brag. All such boasting is evil. Anyone, then, who knows the good he ought to do and doesn't do it, sins (4:1-17).

Self-consumed and self-focused living is a problem everyone else has. That's not a misprint. It's a problem *everyone else* has—very few of us are willing to own up to it in our own lives. If you need help with this, I can give you a hand. After all, I'm really good at pointing out how this shortcoming of selfishness is evident and clear in virtually everyone's life. For example, I have friends who will spend thousands on those flat screen TVs that I covet and crave. I do find great satisfaction knowing that I've never been that self-oriented. As a matter of fact, virtually everything I have is a necessity, not a selfish desire. Sarcasm set aside . . . isn't this how we think? If we want it, we find a way to make sure we can say we "need" it. Once it's a need, we can establish quickly why God wants me to have my basic needs.

This kind of self-orientation is harmful enough to our personal lives and our families. However, when we walk through the church doors and bring those concepts and ideas with us into the body of Christ, we bring something that is ultimately lethal within the body of Christ. Very few divisions in the church have taken place because of legitimate points of doctrine in the last 100 years. The vast majority of divisions come from the same thinking that James confronts. "What causes fights and quarrels among you? Don't they come from your desires that battle within you? You want something but don't get it. You kill and covet, but you cannot have what you want. You quarrel and fight."

> Very few divisions in the last 100 years have been for legitimate points of doctrine.

A friend of mine visited a congregation he had known for many years. He frequently had been invited to speak or teach for their services and classes. However, he noticed a difference on this visit. As he walked into their large auditorium designed to seat 1,500 people, he noticed only three hundred were in attendance. Church members explained to him that the congregation had such a division when it came to worship style that they finally reached a compromise. Those who preferred traditional worship services retained use of the auditorium while those who preferred more modern, expressive worship had been granted use of the gym. The auditorium was filled with godly men and women who had great minds and hearts, but they insisted on preserving their preferred style of worship. The gym was packed to the point of standing room only. These godly men and women also had great minds and hearts, but they too insisted on their preferred style of worship. The comment from my friend has stayed in my mind, "I couldn't help but wonder if these two groups didn't have something valuable to offer each other."

This "personal preference" mind-set plagues congregations whether liberal or conservative, contemporary or traditional. Wherever self-centered agendas are allowed to take root, destruction is close at hand. We want something, we demand something, we insist on our way, and when we don't get it, what do we do? Well, we throw a temper tantrum in order to get the grease promised to the squeakiest wheel on the gospel train. The problem is that God never made that promise (even though it's often been our practice).

> Wherever self-centered agendas are allowed to take root, destruction is close at hand.

James helps us get to the root of the problem by addressing the issue directly. We don't get what we want primarily because of three things: We're not asking God for what we want. We are motivated by the wrong desires. And we want the wrong things. I would never want to question the authority of James's writing abilities, but let's put these in reverse order for our discussion.

Problem number one: *we want the wrong things.* It didn't take me very many months in full-time ministry to realize just how true this is. And it's not that we want the really important wrong things. Most of the time, we want the really trivial, insignificant wrong things. We want a worship experience that better fits our style. We want a church atmosphere that better suits our ideas of dress and appearance. We want a congregational energy level that best matches our own energy level (anything more or less makes me look out of step). We want uniformity instead of unity.

What about Me?

The irony of these trivial issues is the amount of time required of the leadership to deal with them, causing them to neglect some really big "I-want" issues that could genuinely destroy lives. Take, for example, the situation when a married person says, "I want a divorce." All too often I have seen a spouse leave a marriage, mortgaging all familial peace in order to suppress the overwhelming loneliness and guilt that keeps him or her awake at night. Instead of having time to pray with and encourage this brother or sister in Christ, the shepherds are debating whether rhythmic clapping should be forbidden in order to keep five or six members from cornering them week after week.

The list goes on and on when it comes to our self-driven pursuits that walk into our fellowship with us—and consequently destroy the fellowship we enjoy. Americans are some of the whiniest people on the face of the earth. We're also some of the most demanding. When you bring this attitude into the body of Christ, it's immediately detrimental.

Problem number two: *we are motivated by the wrong desires.* Instead of emulating the characteristic of Christ that says, "I'll die on a cross for you," we tend to embrace a modified motto, "I need you to sacrifice for me." What should motivate each of us (and I'm preaching at me as much as anyone) is the desire to take up our cross rather than stand on our personal soap box.

Paul stated this idea best in 2 Corinthians when he comments over and over that he'll boast about his right to build them up instead of tear them down. When was the last time you heard someone fight for their right to encourage and comfort others with no regard for themselves or the greater good of the body? Usually, when the tone is abrasive, so are the words. This comes from a motivation of self-preservation and self-concern rather than genuine concern for others and their needs.

This leads, I believe, to **the last (or first?) problem** introduced by James: *you don't have because you don't ask God.* Why don't we ask God if we really want it? I think it's because we know inherently that what we want doesn't mesh with God's desires and that our motives aren't right in the first place. This is why I like to consider these problems in reverse order. Before we ask God for something, we need to consider if it's something God wants us to have. If it's in sync with God's word and God's desire, we need to make sure our motivation is selfless—like Christ. Now it's time to get on our knees and ask and ask and ask.

When we live this way, self-motivated instead of cross-inspired, we live with no peace. We cannot have peace when we place ourselves at the center of the universe. We can only have peace when we

> When we live self-motivated instead of cross-inspired lives, we have no peace.

live in the world God created, encouraging the people God called, desiring—like Christ—to impact them all with love and encouragement.

We all see the problem of self-centered existence when we look at the sad state of political affairs in the world. Nations are constantly jockeying for what's "theirs" or what "preserves their way of life." You never hear one nation protecting what's best for their neighbor unless it benefits them personally. There is no selflessness. The same is true with the politicians running our world. Under the guise of being public servants, they pursue personal agendas and will make virtually any compromise if it accelerates their pursuit of power.

These are all good examples that are largely impersonal to us. But what happens when we face the selfishness in our families and marriages? What changes when we consider our materialistic pursuits? What comes to mind when we consider the behavior of so many churches that we've been part of? What hits us between the eyes when we think about the arguments between parents and children that spring from selfish interests?

James makes it clear that our lack of peace comes primarily because of our friendship with the world. Friends influence and change us. When we embrace friendship with a self-absorbed world, we become self-absorbed people. The world is kind of like the "bad boy" that all the girls want to date but should never marry. You know the type: cute, cut, and clever. You'd never want to spend your life with him, but he's so much more attractive than the nerdy physics major that sits down the pew from you during communion.

> Our lack of peace comes from of our friendship with the world.

Some time ago, I met a Christian woman who had been dumped by the "cute, cut and clever" and was dating – for no better term – a nice, nerdy computer nut. When I asked about her switch from one to the other, she commented, "I lived a miserable life with the guy every girl wants. I'm going the nerd this time."

Now, I don't want to portray the church as a nerd and the world as a good-looking jock. But some similarities exist. Everybody seems to want to spend time with the world while believing the relationship won't affect personal morals, beliefs, desires, or priorities. The faithless nature of the world eventually leaves us empty and betrayed. On the other hand we are offered a faithful relationship that is fulfilling (and for that matter, very exciting and adventuresome).

If we want the peace, we have to be willing to make some basic changes in the core of who we are. We can do this by fighting off friendship with the world by having two characteristics the world doesn't handle well: humility and courageous living. Humility to put others first and the courage to know that God will give us all the grace and love we need. Humility and self-absorption don't go well together and are repellant to one another.

Another way we can accomplish a healthier, Christlike relationship with the world and with the church is to learn to love and not to leverage. The world constantly uses people for leverage and the opportunity to get ahead. Jesus used love as an opportunity to change lives forever. The world may admire this quality from the observation point across the room, but in the end will reject the notion as an ineffective business plan that only allows others to trample on you. All we have to do is look at the cross to know that this is true. But Jesus humbled himself before the Lord and God exalted him.

How urgent is this matter? James wrote, "What's your life? You are a mist that appears for a little while and then vanishes." We need to remember our mortality and take a moment to reflect on our inability to live forever. We tend to "live it up" in a way that's not "lifting others up." People who invest in others die without regret. They die in the arms of God and often in the arms of those they've loved.

James's reminder on this point should give us urgency: if you know what's right to do and you don't do it, then for you it's sin. We put off cross-shaped living for just this moment because, after all, I deserve it . . . I've earned it. The moment becomes a minute then an hour and soon a day, a week, a lifestyle. None of us intend to do it; we just fall into it because one of our dearest friends—the world—reminds us that we should. The result is the procrastination of selfless living. The result is self-inflicted destruction and division. We don't like it. We want to break off the relationship but don't want to deal with it today. James doesn't suggest, "There's no time like the present." He cuts to the chase and says, "There is no time *except* the present." 3:18

Rising to Perfection

1. If you had to identify three kinds of selfishness that you notice in others the most, what would they be? What types of self-orientation do you witness most?

2. If you had to identify three kinds of selfishness that hamper your own life, what could you identify as three that tempt you or distract you?

3. In what ways is friendship with the world attractive to you? In what ways is friendship with God more important to you?

4. Why do you think it takes courage to live a humble, selfless life? Why does a humble life require faith in God?

5. What have you delayed taking care of? How does this kind of procrastination invite sin into your life?

6. In the context of these teachings of James, we know that we must do the right thing now. If you could do one thing right now that would positively impact your spiritual life simply by acting with urgency, what would it be?

Memory Verse James 4:8-10

Come near to God and he will come near to you. Wash your hands, you sinners, and purify your hearts, you double-minded. Grieve, mourn and wail. Change your laughter to mourning and your joy to gloom. Humble yourselves before the Lord, and he will lift you up.

CHAPTER NINE

WEALTH WARNINGS

JAMES 5:1-6

In 2006 nonprofit charities announced that California was first among the United States when it came to making money and controlling money. However, when it came to giving money to good causes and charities, they fell to 22nd. Living here, I'm sure the reason is *not* that Californians can't bear to part with their money. As a matter of fact, spending money is as much of a fad as it is a necessity in this state driven by entertainment, pleasure, and the enjoyment of life. However, there is a noticeable emptiness in the #1 money state in the #1 money nation in the world. Despite the fact that this one state is the sixth largest economy in the world, it's also home to millions of empty lives and people looking for something that will make them feel like they're really living.

Because of our national wealth and moral bankruptcy, James 5:1-6 is worth a couple of looks from a couple of different angles. Here's what he says:

> Now listen, you rich people, weep and wail because of the misery that is coming upon you. Your wealth has rotted, and moths have eaten your clothes. Your gold and silver are corroded. Their corrosion will testify against you and eat your flesh like fire. You have hoarded wealth in the last days. Look! The wages you failed to pay the workmen who mowed your fields are crying out against you. The cries of the harvesters have reached the ears of the Lord Almighty. You have lived on earth in luxury and self-indulgence. You have fattened your-

selves in the day of slaughter. You have condemned and murdered innocent men, who were not opposing you.

If we considered these words to be a house, we can see that perspective changes depending on where you're standing. For example, if you look into my home through the front window, you get a completely different view than if you look into our house through the side window. The same is true with these words of James. We'll look through the window of "warnings" first and then the window of "worship" in the next chapter.

The background of these verses is important but a little elusive. We know from the prophets, the life of Jesus, the Gospel of Luke, and from our relationship with God that our Creator has an affection and love for the poor. He sees those who suffer because of neglect and marginalization through eyes of compassion. He seeks for those of us who can do something about it financially to step up and do what we can.

> **Our Creator has an affection and love for the poor; he seeks for us to do what we can to help.**

While James has been writing to believers up to this point about issues specific to the believers' treatment of one another, he now turns to address an issue that is witnessed every day by those Jewish Christians who suffer at the hands of the politically protected and connected. We know from history that the Roman authorities and Jewish powers oppressed the early church in every way they could—including financially. The church in Jerusalem came to be known as "the poor" and Paul spent much of his time and efforts encouraging financial gifts on their behalf (1 Corinthians 16, 2 Corinthians 8–10).

When we read the opening words of James 5, our immediate tendency is to take one of two paths. The first is to rightfully interpret the passages as directly related to the financial powers of the world that are oppressing the early church. The second approach is to interpret the message as written about and to those wealthy Christians in the church who aren't raising a finger to help their brethren (not the preferred interpretation by most scholars).

I believe that we need to blend the two approaches because of our status as wealthy Christians. We have such high financial status compared to the world around us that we are tempted to oppress the poor through ignorance or indifference. We end up with a nagging awareness tucked in the back of our spiritual minds that we may in fact be the oppressors. On the flip side, our culture is becoming more and more combative towards people of faith. We could easily end up being financially oppressed in a rerun of historical disdain for people of

Christian conviction. Before we blindly move forward with our materialistic cultural norms, we need to back up and develop some self-awareness in this regard.

James issues seven specific wealth warnings that I notice in this passage. Some of them are complete and straightforward. Some of them are implied. Whether they're exposed or floating below the surface, we need to take them to heart in light of our existence as people of great wealth and people of God.

1. Wealthy people have a responsibility to use their wealth for God's purposes. As a matter of fact, the sooner we come to grips with the fact that it's not our wealth at all, the sooner we'll find ourselves understanding and enjoying the wealth we've been entrusted with.
2. Wealth doesn't last forever, it corrodes.
3. Wealth corrodes those who hoard it.
4. Those who hoard destroy those who threaten the stash of cash.
5. God hears those who are suffering and will eventually correct the imbalance.
6. If you live in luxury and self-indulgence, you're fattening yourself up for a physical and painful day of slaughter.
7. Money tempts those who have it to self-protect at the cost of others who aren't even their real enemies.

Warning One: Responsibility with Wealth

Minister and mentor, Dr. Lynn Anderson, was told by a friend of his that 5% of the wealthiest people in the world were looking for the 5% of ministers in the world who really want to make a difference so they could invest their money in doing something good. These wealthy Christians understand something many have difficulty grasping: Money is a tool given to people in order to accomplish good. Just like any other blessing, what God intends for good, Satan manipulates for evil. James calls the financially corrupt to account throughout his letter. Just as the Law given to the Israelites called for a sacrifice covering unknown sins, which are sins committed unintentionally; we need to be aware that we can unintentionally be corrupt with our wealth.

We can easily begin to think that wealth is primarily given to us for our own pleasure and enjoyment. However, God gives us wealth in order that he can be pleased through watching his children use wealth as a way to bless others as well as ourselves.

> God gives us wealth so that he can be pleased watching us use it to bless others.

One of our young fathers recently told our congregation a story about his son and a gift he gave him. He had given his child money and watched as the money was eagerly placed in the contribution plate during a church service. The idea was simple and profound. His child didn't earn the money—it was a gift. When the child immediately gave the gift away to others, the father was pleased. This young man is a father like our God—he derives joy from watching the generosity of his children.

God doesn't demand his children live in poverty because they give sacrificially, but self-impoverished people are like God's son Jesus. Jesus willingly left heaven and came to earth to live as the son of a carpenter and to be a wandering preacher for three years of his life before dying on a cross with thieves. He was faithfully willing to use his position in creation in order to help others. Do we do the same?

> Jesus was willing to use his position in creation to help others. Do we do the same?

Warning Two: Wealth Corrodes

This is more challenging to grasp because of our modern monetary system. There was a day when silver and gold coins were the currency of the day. I have a coin collection from my childhood. In it are a number of "valuable" coins. However, no coin was more valuable to me than an 1890s half-dime. This coin was used before the nickel existed. I've kept that coin since I found it in high school. A year ago, I took my coin collection out to see how it was doing after three moves and more than a decade. The half-dime is literally fading away. You can barely see it's original markings at all. Time is taking its toll and corroding the coin.

We don't see money corrode too much any more. I'm more likely to have a credit card crack because of overuse than I am coins corrode. However, we know what it's like to have money come and go faster than expected. We know what it's like to spend a ton of money on a car only to have it break down and depreciate so fast that we are still, ". . . paying for this piece of junk." We see that the "stuff" we purchase with our money falls apart. No matter what you do, possessions you purchase and money you have will not stand the test of time.

Warning Three: Wealth Corrodes Those Who Hoard It

The corrosion sadly doesn't end with a coin; it continues deep into the soul. When the first wealth warning isn't taken to heart, it begins to destroy the heart. The world acknowledges this and tries to deal with the issue in secular stories like Scrooge, Pretty Woman, and Wall Street.

The common thread in these stories is a wealthy person who works to amass more wealth in order to amass even more wealth. It destroys their lives. It destroys their relationships. It takes away from them the very thing they are trying to get their hands on—abundant life. If the world sees this and writes endless stories about it, why do we have such difficulty grasping it ourselves? After all, wealth promises something that only God can deliver. We believe by having money we can experience the abundant life Jesus promised us in John 10:10. Ironically, money can take life right out of our hands. In each of these stories, the primary victim of the wealth is the person who has the wealth.

Warning Four: Those Who Hoard Destroy Others

Slightly different from warning three is warning four (but the slight difference is still significant). What do you do when you have $1,000,000,000.00 (that's a lot of zeroes)? You want more from those around you. Living in Sacramento, California, is addictive for sports fans because we are home to the Sacramento Kings (some would say this won't last long . . . but who knows). The saga of the Kings in 2006 is a great example of this.

The Maloof family owns the Palms hotel in Las Vegas. They are also majority owners of the Sacramento Kings. In 2006, they starred in a Carl's Junior commercial that was aired throughout the Western United States. The commercial, which was filmed at the Maloof's casino in Las Vegas, promoted a $6,000 meal that included a $6.00 burger and a $6,000 bottle of fine, aged wine. At the same time the commercial was released, the voters in Sacramento were being asked to decide on increasing local sales taxes in order to generate enough money to build a new arena for the Kings. Many cited the commercial as one of the major factors for the ballot measure being defeated.

In all of the discussions surrounding the issue is a reality of our world: Rich people are rich because they make decisions that help them amass wealth rather than reduce wealth. The commercial stated the net worth of the Maloof brothers as one billion dollars. To build a new arena would cost half that. Why not build the arena? Because they're good businessmen who know that they don't need to when cities around the U.S. are begging them to come with no financial liabilities. It's the promise of making even more money than they do in Sacramento.

Bottom line: those who have money do everything they can to keep others from having it. They work and plan in order to increase their wealth because that's what they do. However, while amassing more wealth for themselves, they also demand greater sacrifice from those who aren't as financially blessed. Every now and then, someone bucks the system and the system doesn't know how to handle it. Bill Gates, founder and owner of Microsoft, makes the Maloof brothers look broke. Gates has decided that he'll leave a small fortune to his children and give the rest away to charities. He's bringing other billionaires around to this kind of thinking. The problem is that it's countercultural and while people admire him for it, they don't apply the same idea personally. In most cases, though, the wealthy don't mind getting wealthier at the expense of the masses of less fortunate around them.

When we talk about wealthy people, most Americans think we're talking about someone else. What about those of us who think we're not wealthy but just don't realize just how good we've got it? We assume that if we had Gates's money we'd do the same. The problem is that we're not called to be faithful with his money; we're called to be faithful with God's money that's on loan to us. Do we use our money for us or for God? Do we leverage our wealth to lift us up while holding others down?

> We are not called to be faithful with Bill Gates's money but our own.

Warning Five: God Hears the Suffering

Not much needs to be said about this other than these words of truth: God causes nations to rise and fall. While it cannot be said that God will bring wealth to the faithful, it is true that he will eventually strip away the wealth of those who use it against his kingdom and his cause. The departure of the Israelites out of Egypt is the perfect example of this. God heard their cry, and once he decided to free his people, no amount of money or power could defeat the power of God.

Many nations around the world (including the United States of America) need to pay attention to this. You want God and faith out of your nation? Be careful, you'll eventually get what you're asking for, and when God replies, "Fine, then you can see what it's like without me," you'll regret the day you made that decision. This isn't a threat, it's a fact. God has a heart for the oppressed and will respond to their cries. When his people or a nation takes care of the oppressed, it pleases God. It's our responsibility to be like God and care for the oppressed.

Warning Six: You Are the Fattened Calf

I really don't like what James is saying here, but it is Scripture, and we ought to think about it. When people ignore warnings one through five, they end up with warning six being one of their last two chances for correction. He wants us to know that you can live in luxury and self-indulgence to the point where you become the perfect sacrifice. Most of us can't imagine ever slaughtering a sacrificial lamb on the altar. However, the people of Israel knew this experience and the imagery made sense.

The livestock used for sacrifice were the ones with the most meat on their bones. They had been fattened for one purpose: sacrifice to God. Well, James looks around the farm that is the world and notices several fattened calves—those who have fattened themselves at the expense of others—and sees the perfect sacrifice.

If we live in luxury and self-indulgence, it's like a spiritual and physical death wish. I know what you're thinking, "This sounds too much like Old Testament prophecy stuff and that doesn't apply any more." Well, guess what, we need to listen to the words of the prophets like never before and pay attention to prophetic language when it comes up in the New Testament. James resurrects this language when he points out that a day of slaughter is coming for those who hoard wealth in the very presence of the impoverished.

> We need to listen more to the words of the prophets and prophetic language in the NT.

Final Warning: Money Tempts Us to Self-protect

Wealth is so deceptive and the love of money so powerful that we can find ourselves being ugly to people around us that aren't even our enemies. James knew this was going on in his culture. He cited the rich people who abused the oppressed in fear that their wealth would be diminished. While James doesn't expand on this problem in detail, we do know that they used their wealth against people who weren't even a threat to them or their wealth. Why? Money causes a deep kind of paranoia that's not healthy.

How many stories like Howard Hughes need to be told before we realize that wealth can cause you to become a recluse who has no trust for anyone or anything? It's the story of a thousand celebrities we've read about. It's the story of virtually every person who's won the lottery. Once we reach a certain level of wealth, we begin to think that everyone's after our money. Why do you think we have an entire legal profession built around prenuptial agreements?

So what's the problem with that? Isn't it just good business? Isn't this fiscal responsibility? Isn't this the way business is done? I leave you with one thought that answers the question clearly: Where would man be if God chose to self-protect? ⌷

Rising to Perfection

1. In what ways are you good with money? What have you used your money for that signified in your life that you were behaving like God?

2. In what ways do you use money that are not so godly?

3. What amount of money would it take to have in your bank for you to think, "I've arrived, I'm now rich."

4. Of the seven wealth warnings, which warning do you need to really take to heart?

5. In what ways do you see that God does the opposite of "self-protect"? Write down some Scriptures or Bible stories that illustrate this?

Memory Verse
James 5:1-3

Now listen, you rich people, weep and wail because of the misery that is coming upon you. Your wealth has rotted, and moths have eaten your clothes. Your gold and silver are corroded. Their corrosion will testify against you and eat your flesh like fire. You have hoarded wealth in the last days.

CHAPTER TEN

WEALTH WORSHIP

JAMES 5:1-6

We need to consider another aspect of wealth. In Chapter 9 we considered the warnings that James issues in chapter five. Certainly these verses are filled with warnings:

> Now listen, you rich people, weep and wail because of the misery that is coming upon you. Your wealth has rotted, and moths have eaten your clothes. Your gold and silver are corroded. Their corrosion will testify against you and eat your flesh like fire. You have hoarded wealth in the last days. Look! The wages you failed to pay the workmen who mowed your fields are crying out against you. The cries of the harvesters have reached the ears of the Lord Almighty. You have lived on earth in luxury and self-indulgence. You have fattened yourselves in the day of slaughter. You have condemned and murdered innocent men, who were not opposing you (5:1-6).

James gives Christians a direction for our praise and admiration: don't worship wealth, worship God.

This is difficult in a land where the loudest, most prominent ministers we know preach a health and wealth gospel. "If you believe in Jesus, he'll bless you with health and wealth." Try telling the devoted Christian father dying of cancer this message. Try explaining that gospel to the Christian mother who lives in a third-world country and watches her children starve. The good news of Jesus isn't health and wealth, it's abundant living *in the face of* suffering or unjust circumstances. Some are afforded life in safety and abundance, and God expects more from those blessed in this manner. Some survive in the worst of circumstances, and God has a special place in His heart for those who suffer in this way. He also wants to see how the one can help the other. Can the "have's" reach out to the "have not's" both spiritually and physically? James knows we *can*, he wants to make sure we *will*.

> James knows the "have's" can reach out to the "have not's"; he wants to make sure they will.

That said, it all comes down to this: What do we worship? Who is on the throne of our heart? Who sits as Lord of our life and who do we exalt in worship?

Worship is defined as the "Human response to the perceived presence of the divine, a presence which transcends normal human activity and is holy" (*Holman Bible Dictionary*). The key word is "response." You can tell from the response of people what they worship. They lift it up, they protect it, they admire it, they . . . well, they worship it. The number one thing worshiped in our culture is money. I know that sexuality and entertainment are near the top of the list, but money is what sits on the throne of our hearts more than any other. It's money that usually gives credibility to the sexual and entertainment celebrities that we worship.

Jesus said, "God is spirit, and his worshipers must worship in spirit and in truth" (John 4:24). We are called to worship with energy ("in spirit" can be translated *with charisma*) and integrity (in truth). That energy can be expressed in many different ways. For example, what Solomon writes in Ecclesiastes 5:1-2:

> Guard your steps when you go to the house of God. Go near to listen rather than to offer the sacrifice of fools, who do not know that they do wrong. Do not be quick with your mouth, do not be hasty in your heart to utter anything before God. God is in heaven and you are on earth, so let your words be few.

In this text energy and integrity are captured in quiet reflection and listening. This is seen in another great story of Scripture. When Elijah was depleted of his energy and faith, God needed to restore his strength and hope. Elijah experienced a moment of worship with God that gives us insight into God and his character.

> The LORD said, "Go out and stand on the mountain in the presence of the LORD, for the LORD is about to pass by." Then a great and powerful wind tore the mountains apart and shattered the rocks before the LORD, but the LORD was not in the wind. After the wind there was an earthquake, but the LORD was not in the earthquake. After the earthquake came a fire, but the LORD was not in the fire. And after the fire came a

gentle whisper. When Elijah heard it, he pulled his cloak over his face and went out and stood at the mouth of the cave (1 Kgs 19:11-13).

That "worship energy" discovered in Elijah's moment with God is reflected in much different forms in other moments of worship. Notice in Psalm 47:

> Clap your hands, all you nations;
>> shout to God with cries of joy.
> How awesome is the LORD Most High,
>> the great King over all the earth!
> He subdued nations under us,
>> peoples under our feet.
> He chose our inheritance for us,
>> the pride of Jacob, whom he loved.
>
> *Selah*
>
> God has ascended amid shouts of joy,
>> the LORD amid the sounding of trumpets.
> Sing praises to God, sing praises;
>> sing praises to our King, sing praises.
> For God is the King of all the earth;
>> sing to him a psalm of praise.
> God reigns over the nations;
>> God is seated on his holy throne.
> The nobles of the nations assemble
>> as the people of the God of Abraham,
> for the kings of the earth belong to God;
>> he is greatly exalted (Ps 47:1-9).

In this Psalm of praise and worship the call for energy comes through clapping, shouting, crying, singing, and assembling with others. For Elijah it was a whisper. In Ecclesiastes it is through quietness before the Lord. These are all called-for responses in Scripture (and we could list others with virtually no end). These physical expressions or responses are consistently seen throughout Scripture from Genesis through Revelation.

I have seen the same responses in our culture with one marked difference: the subject of the worship.

> *We applaud for rich athletes making in one game more than most earn in a year.*
>
> *We shout praises to celebrities and athletes and throw money in worship of them when we purchase our tickets.*
>
> *We cry out in hopes that they will notice us from among the crowd.*
>
> *We sing songs about money and the love of money that we so desire.*
>
> *We gather in many assemblies around our nation seeking input on how to get more money.*

We stand in awe of money. Only the bank is as quiet as the library. It's almost as contemplative as a communion service on Sunday.
We protect it, hide it, admire it, etc., etc., etc.

We are tempted to worship money, the things it buys, and the people who have it. Why? We love it, want it, and seek it every day of our lives.

Recently I was visiting with members as they prepared to visit Health Talent's International clinic in Guatemala. My daughter was traveling with the group and I wanted as much information as I could get. One young man approached me and told me he'd been a couple of times. He conveyed that in previous years those help-ing stayed with families in the local communities rather than in the upscale clinic housing that had been recently added. He lamented that fact since his life was changed by his stay. The family that kept him and his friend owned a one-room house that was basically a sleep shelter. The father of the family had an annual income of less than three hun-dred dollars! In other words, these two college students carried with them more money than this family would see in several years.

> **We are tempted to worship money, the things it buys, and the people who have it.**

When my daughter returned, one of her highlights was the day they spent in the local communities seeing the people. She noticed how strong the ties were in the communities. Everyone was outdoors together. They cooked outside as a community. Their children played together in the streets. They worked together in the fields. In other words, they were living abundant lives in conditions we wouldn't accept for a weekend camping trip.

How can this be? We stand, just like the Grinch from Dr. Seuss's famous story, on the materialistic peak of Mt. Crumpett, holding all the wealth of the world around us and can't comprehend how the people can still sing on Christmas morning without all the stuff. How can they live without the TV and microwave? How can they sing songs without projectors and PowerPoint? How can they rejoice without I-PODs and laptops? How can they experience joy in the face of poverty? They value, they worship, they respond without the wealth.

We worship wealth in four key ways.

We Worship by Hoarding

Each year I have to spend about four days of my life reorganizing all the junk that I keep in my garage. Part of this is because of our iso-lated and redundant living. For example, everyone on my street owns his own lawn mower and has to make room for it. It doesn't matter that we'd all gladly loan our neighbor our mower for the fifteen minutes it takes to mow a lawn in California. That's not the point. We have to have our own.

All our possessions are like idols that we carry into the Promised Land. They weigh us down physically and spiritually, but we don't want to let them go. This hoarding or collecting is simply a modern version of idol worship. We buy stuff, and then allow it to control our lives. Through this we become cluttered spiritually. Our hearts begin to look like our garages.

We Worship by Charging

Jesus told a very short parable about this. "The kingdom of heaven is like treasure hidden in a field. When a man found it, he hid it again, and then in his joy went and sold all he had and bought that field" (Matt 13:44). The man wanted something so badly that he leveraged everything he could to own it. We do the same every day with our credit cards and home equity loans.

The problem is that we don't leverage everything we have for a great treasure; we leverage everything in order to own an item that's mass produced for sale at an incredible markup worldwide in order that we can be just like the people down the street from us. To add insult to injury, we're leveraging what we don't have in order to own what we don't need. In this way, we worship wealth. We'll give anything for it.

> We're leveraging what we don't have in order to own what we don't need.

We Worship by Watching

Let me state the obvious—the TV is the favored object of worship for our modern world (and not just in America). This is a worldwide, idolatrous epidemic. It's probably my greatest personal weakness and source of envy. Every time I walk into Sam's or Costco I am drawn to the display of the flat screen TVs.

If we purchased one, it would make sense. After all, our family room can only hold four people comfortably. Since God desires that we be a hospitable people, we could expand our abilities to open our home to others if our family room could hold eight people comfortably instead of four. To do this, we'd need to remove our huge, bulky entertainment center. As a matter of fact, by purchasing the flat-panel HDTV, we would actually de-emphasize the place of TV in our lives and probably make a great statement of faith to people in our homes.

We could even put a "spiritual screen saver" as a background so that people would be encouraged in their faith just sitting in our *TV* room . . . oops . . . our *family* room.

You can tell I've really thought this rationalization through and played with every possible way to justify getting this new toy. Now some are going to make a point that buying an HDTV isn't a sin and can have real value. True. The problem is we don't just use them, we live by them. We worship them.

Recently churches have seen a sharp decline in Sunday evening and Wednesday evening gatherings. The usual rationale is that families need more time together since their commuting lives are so busy. The problem is that I know what most families do with this family time—they watch the tube. It has replaced the telling of daily stories and has long since taken precedence over the discussion of God's word in our homes. The bottom line is that our schedules have more TV time in them than God time.

> Our schedules have more TV time in them than God time.

We Worship by Admiring

A friend of mine was working in the Dallas area when he got invited to a Dallas Mavericks game (the local basketball team). My friend made one of the most profound comments I've heard. He said that during the game people were going crazy, shouting, screaming, clapping, cheering and in that moment he thought, "I am among my people and they are worshiping their God."

Their god wasn't the Dallas Mavericks. Their god is the god of most of our society—money, power, and entertainment. We don't just enjoy it. Our energetic response rises to the level of worship. Our admiration has risen to a level of inspiration that is spiritually disgusting. Believers who would never raise a hand or song in praise to God shout at the top of their ability in order to worship a different god, one that isn't a god at all.

Notice how easy it is and how natural Psalm 47 sounds with this setting inserted:

Clap your hands, every fan;
   shout with cries of joy.
How awesome is the team we have,
   and notice how they own all the other teams!
They subdued the Nets and the Knicks
   as if they put their feet on their throats.
They chose this city as their home,
   and we are their fans.

They've risen through the ranks
    and ascended amid shouts of joy;
we enjoy pounding music
    as they take the court.
Join in with the team dancers
    as we scream their name and praises.
For they will win the championship this year;
    we should praise the wealthy owners
    who provide us with this joy.
Everybody who's anybody
    is here at these games,
and they aren't embarrassed
    to let it all hang out
    to cheer their team.
May they be praised forever!

Some take this and say, "That's exactly why we don't worship God that way. That's for NBA teams and football games . . . not for God." That's exactly backwards. That kind of energy and enthusiasm isn't for people or stuff or things; it's supposed to be reserved for God, and we channel it in every direction except toward God.

I can't give you an easy, step-by-step solution or tell you how to balance these issues in your life because I haven't figured it out for my life either. This I can say: we need to shift our worship and admiration away from the idols and gods of our culture and focus that energy and integrity back towards God. Only he is truly worthy of our praise!

> We must shift our worship and admiration away from the idols and gods of our culture

Rising to Perfection

1. Share a moment when you could make the same statement as my friend, "I am among my people, and they are worshiping their God."

2. When do you most notice people worshiping the god of money and materialism?

3. What "thing" do you want so badly that you can't get it out of your mind?

4. Why do you want this "thing" so badly? What do you believe it will provide for you? What emptiness do you hope it will fulfill or complete?

5. What about God do you truly desire? What do you believe God will provide for you that is fulfilling?

6. What specific thing can you do to turn your worship tendencies away from the world and back towards God?

Memory Verses

James 5:5
Eccl 5:1-2

You have lived on earth in luxury and self-indulgence. You have fattened yourselves in the day of slaughter.

Guard your steps when you go to the house of God. Go near to listen rather than to offer the sacrifice of fools, who do not know that they do wrong. Do not be quick with your mouth, do not be hasty in your heart to utter anything before God. God is in heaven and you are on earth, so let your words be few.

CHAPTER ELEVEN

VIBRANT FAITH FROM BEGINNING TO END

JAMES 5:7-20

Every Christian I know wants to have vibrant faith; a faith that hopes in the midst of despair and acts in the face of opposition. For all the discussion about James being a letter of nuts and bolts Christianity—just the do's and don'ts—it seems to me that James the Apostle has been misjudged and misinterpreted in this regard. After all, James begins and ends with one call for God's people—pray:

Be patient, then, brothers, until the Lord's coming. See how the farmer waits for the land to yield its valuable crop and how patient he is for the autumn and spring rains. You too, be patient and stand firm, because the Lord's coming is near. Don't grumble against each other, brothers, or you will be judged. The Judge is standing at the door!

Brothers, as an example of patience in the face of suffering, take the prophets who spoke in the name of the Lord. As you know, we consider blessed those who have persevered. You have heard of Job's perseverance and have seen what the Lord finally brought about. The Lord is full of compassion and mercy.

Above all, my brothers, do not swear—not by heaven or by earth or by anything else. Let your "Yes" be yes, and your "No," no, or you will be condemned. Is any one of you in trouble? He should pray. Is anyone happy? Let him sing songs of praise.

Is any one of you sick? He should call the elders of the church to pray over him and anoint him with oil in the name of the Lord. And the prayer offered in faith will make the sick person well; the Lord will raise him up. If he has sinned, he will be forgiven. Therefore confess your sins to each other and pray for each other so that you may be healed. The prayer of a righteous man is powerful and effective.

Elijah was a man just like us. He prayed earnestly that it would not rain, and it did not rain on the land for three and a half years. Again he prayed, and the heavens gave rain, and the earth produced its crops.

My brothers, if one of you should wander from the truth and someone should bring him back, remember this: Whoever turns a sinner from the error of his way will save him from death and cover over a multitude of sins (5:7-20).

The first message James delivered centered on those who desire wisdom. He didn't say, "Go get a master's degree and you'll have wisdom"; he said, "If any of you lacks wisdom, he should ask God, who gives generously to all without finding fault, and it will be given to him" (Jas 1:5).

He opens with a call to prayer (specifically a prayer for wisdom) and closes with a call to prayer (specifically prayer for healing). Although, I think in focusing on the prayer for healing we miss the overarching emphasis of James: you can't have vibrant faith on your own; you're going to have to depend on God. You also can't have a vibrant church without the same attitude of prayer.

> **You can't have vibrant faith on your own; you're going to have to depend on God.**

Have you noticed how churches argue over the silliest things? I mean consider all the things that have caused serious division in the church. We have divided over building designs, leadership structures, worship preferences, and these are some of the more noble arguments. I think it might be a good practice for us to picture ourselves at the foot of the cross while we're debating church issues and allow that setting to determine if the battle we're fighting is what Christ died for. You rarely hear churches split over the desire for more prayer (although I've had people tell me they don't need to drive to a building in order to pray with other Christians). Rather, we tend to draw lines of fellowship over less noble issues like carpet, clapping, and construction costs.

James jumps right into the middle of our debates and clarifies that our impatience and selfishness are what cause divisions. This is certainly true for me and the churches I've worked with. Guess what? I'm part of the problem like everyone else. For example, I believe there is great value in doing physical acts that have spiritual meaning. Communion is one. We could sit in pews and imagine taking bread or drinking wine, but actually taking it means more because the spiritual is attached by God to the physical. Baptism is the same. It has great spiritual meaning that we could envision with our eyes closed, but experiencing it is something you just don't forget. After all, dying, being buried, and being raised are easily understood in the act of being immersed under the water and brought back up to live a new life. This is another physical act God gave us with spiritual meaning and power.

I would argue that the same is true for kneeling, bowing, lifting holy hands, clapping, shouting, and singing. To me, if you don't do it, you don't get it. However, I'm aware that many of my brothers in Christ view these things as pure emotionalism that is to be avoided at virtually all costs. Yes, they see the value in communion and baptism but stop there when it comes to physical examples from the Bible.

In my impatience, I get frustrated that we seem to never move forward. In their impatience they get frustrated with any changes in this regard at all. I'm ready to move forward, and they are ready for a complete retreat. If we're not careful, the issue will turn from the legitimate question, "How do we worship in spirit and truth—with energy and integrity?" to a question much less legitimate, "What can you do to keep me happy?"

What makes me nervous is James's conclusion about the impatience and selfishness that cause the problems: these issues will be settled by God. Sounds like mom's response to the kids fussing and fighting all day, "You just wait 'til your father gets home." In other words, "Your dad is going to settle this once and for all, and it won't be pleasant for any of you."

I don't know why kids tend to grumble against each other, but we know that James's inclusion of the issue means it's been affecting us for at least 2,000 years. The story of Cain and Abel makes it clear that it's been an issue from the beginning. The solution is still the same: be patient and unselfish and trust that God will take care of things.

> Be patient and unselfish and trust that God will take care of things.

This is a bitter pill to swallow for a person who stands in front of the microwave frustrated because it's taking so long to cook lunch. We live in a fast world where decisions have to be made and things have to happen on a moment-by-moment basis. We can communicate faster than ever before, but you'll notice our ability to communicate efficiently hasn't increased our effectiveness when we communicate. How many times does an email get misread and misunderstood and eventually force a face-to-face confrontation? How many times do you just want to throw a cell phone across the room in order to buy a little peace and quiet? Our world and our culture are not prone to patience.

We also aren't big on being unselfish. Perhaps the best example of this is the American church at large. You can pick a church that has your color of people, speaking your native language, looking the same age, worshiping with your preferred style, with your preferred length of sermon while communion is always available from the add-on menu of churchshoppingpreferences.com. You can see how the message from James doesn't get a great deal of time in the pulpits of America.

The question then is how to live together while living for God. Two good examples for Christian living are introduced in these final words. He chooses for exhibit A and B two characters we should all learn from: Job and Elijah. This is an interesting combination for any writer. I could ask the obvious question, "What on earth do those two have in common?" Well, what they share in common is very profound.

First of all, they prayed. I know that Job finally gets frustrated and demands that God hear his complaints. But we need to remember that God commends Job as an example throughout Scripture, so God must not have been too offended. I'm also aware that Elijah ended up exhausted and burnt out and ready to die before God renewed him with a spiritual pick-me-up. Job and Elijah— under stresses that no one wants to ever face—both prayed to God. They were men of prayer. They were men of patient prayer. James says we should pay attention to their examples.

> We should follow the examples of men of patient prayer.

Secondly, they stuck it out. Job sat on an ash heap reflecting on the loss of life in his family and the loss of everything he owned and finally determined that God was not punishing him. Guess what? He was right! Elijah followed God's bloody directions and fought, taught, confronted, and then had to run for his life. He had the most powerful ruler dead set against him but the most powerful God right there behind him. Both men, in the face of despair, rose to the occasion with vibrant faith that leads to prayer and patience.

How could they do this in their circumstances? Well, they depended on God. This is what James is trying to get the church to see: no matter your situation, there is a Godly, Christian response.

When you're in trouble, pray.
When you have a reason to be happy, praise.
When you're sick, call on the elders.
When you've sinned, confess to your Christian friends.
When someone hurts you, forgive because God forgives.
When you're put to the test, believe in the power of prayer and God.
Beginning to end, remember each other.

James slips in a command or at least a directive in these writings that many are uncomfortable with. It's one of those things that falls under the category of physical acts that have a spiritual meaning. He says if you're sick, you should call the elders to pray for you. If you're an elder, you should anoint people with oil and pray for them.

In the fall of 2005 I was contacted by Dr. Jerry Rushford of Pepperdine University with an invitation to serve as a featured speaker at the annual conference held on campus known as the Pepperdine Lectures. I was honored and would never turn such an invitation down. However, I have to admit, when he gave me the title of the sermon, I was less than enthused. He wanted me to preach from 1 John on the topic of, "Spirit-Anointed Fellowship." I have to tell you that my heritage hasn't really equipped me with confidence when it comes to speaking about the Spirit of God. I had never seen anyone anointed and was quite certain the practice was retired for specific and entrenched reasons. Fellowship was the only one of the three that I had experience with. I've eaten at a lot of potlucks so I'm almost an expert at fellowships.

> After lots of potlucks, I'm almost an expert at fellowships.

The next seven months were spent reading and studying about the meaning of these three words and the practices encouraged or commanded by God. During this study, it dawned on me that I would need to both understand and experience anointing if I were going to effectively preach on the topic. My first opportunity came at a worship service just one month after I started my research.

On a Thursday evening in Nashville, Tennessee, I was attending a leadership conference hosted by the worship team known as Zoe. Brandon Scott Thomas, the leader of that group, was hosting a postmodern worship experience that evening, and I made it a priority to be there. During the service several "stations" for interactive worship were made available for the two hundred in attendance. You could stand before a map of the fifteen countries where Christians were being martyred at the highest rates and pray for God's hand to be with his people. You could make your way to a candlelit prayer journaling area. And, you could also be prayed over and anointed by an elder of the church.

I had never met this shepherd who stood at the front of the room. He must have been seventy-five years old or older. He stood with his wife as we filed toward the front. He anointed my forehead with oil and prayed for me with hands on my shoulders. It was both a very spiritual and very physical and very emotional moment. It was worship with "spirit and truth"—with energy and integrity.

This experience converged with my research as I read the historians who largely believe that the power was not in the anointing, but in the prayer. In other words, the act of anointing someone with oil was

93

‡

C
H
A
P
T
E
R

Vibrant Faith from Beginning to End 11

an act of physical soothing. It was a way to minister to the physical needs of the sick. The prayer—offered in faith—was what brought the power of God into the equation. However, to separate the two loses the part that James is equally interested in.

Remember earlier when James wrote, "Suppose a brother or sister is without clothes and daily food. If one of you says to him, 'Go, I wish you well; keep warm and well fed,' but does nothing about his physical needs, what good is it? In the same way, faith by itself, if it is not accompanied by action, is dead" (Jas 2:14-17). You can have faith to pray for someone's needs, but that person also needs you to physically act to help his or her healing process. This is why James tells us to call for the elders.

During these days of preparation one of my friends was recovering from the horrible loss of her daughter to a drunk driver. We prayed for her on a daily basis to heal as much as a parent could after suffering as she had. Almost a year to the date of her tragedy, she became very ill and ended up in the hospital. At several points she was near death.

We gathered for prayers and I headed to the hospital to pray over her in the ICU. When I arrived, the family was in the hall and I was invited to go inside to pray over her. As I spoke to her in her comatose state, the nurse entered the room. My friend was scheduled for an MRI and needed to be wheeled downstairs for the test. The nurse pulled out a hairbrush and began talking to her like everything was just normal.

I watched wondering what on earth this nurse was thinking. Here was a woman on the edge of death one year after losing her daughter, and she was worried about her hair? She brushed it, styled it, let me pray over her and then prepared the bed for departure. As we walked out of the room I was quietly irritated with the triviality of the woman. As the doors to the hall opened, the first thing out of the mouth of the mother and sister was, "Oh, thanks for doing her hair, she would've wanted that done just like that."

I suddenly realized my mistake. All I could think was, "You idiot! You remembered to pray, but you forgot to anoint." That's right, anoint. If I understand the scholars, what the nurse did was a modern form of anointing. In James's day, anointing meant applying soothing oil to the skin and scalp of the infirm. My friend didn't need oils or lotions, but she needed both physical and spiritual care. I prayed but forgot to anoint.

This issue came up again six months later. One of our brothers who served as an elder of the church was riddled with cancer. He had been through every kind of chemo treatment available. He caught me in the aisle the week after we learned his cancer had returned. As I neared him, he whispered in my ear, "I want you to know your elders listen to

94

‡

C
H
A
P
T
E
R

11   *Vibrant Faith from Beginning to End*

your sermons. They came to my house and anointed my head with oil and laid hands of prayer on my shoulders." Whether the cancer leaves or not, that act of faith will go with him into the Promised Land.

Vibrant Faith

Vibrant faith is born when we depend on God and depend on prayer. There is no shortcut program for development of faith. It depends on *living for* and *depending on* God more than anything else. Vibrant faith is seen in the act of kindness to a widow. It's seen in a hospitable greet-

> Vibrant faith is born when we depend on God and on prayer.

ing to a person who walks in the church from off the cold streets. It's witnessed when elders surround a dying Christian to pray over him while anointing him with oil. God sees it when his children get along instead of fighting and fussing. This is vibrant faith. This is faith that draws the lost to the cross and helps them rise to perfection.

When we have this kind of faith and live this faith, we announce to the world that we're wholly given to God as he is wholly given to us. As they are drawn to Jesus, we enjoy the blessing of a changed life and a saved soul. James leaves us with one final word of encouragement designed to draw us into this living faith, "Remember this: Whoever turns a sinner from the error of his way will save him from death and cover over a multitude of sins" (Jas 5:20).

Rising to Perfection

1. Do you tend to be more uncomfortable with progress or with the lack of progress? Why?

2. If you compare yourself to Job and Elijah, which do you identify with more? Are you the one suffering on an ash heap or are you the one who's beaten up from victories that have taken their toll?

3. James speaks about several faith responses listed in this chapter.

   When you're in trouble, pray.
   When you have a reason to be happy, praise.
   When you're sick, call on the elders.
   When you've sinned, confess to your Christian friends.
   When someone hurts you, forgive because God forgives.
   When you're put to the test, believe in the power of prayer and God.
   Beginning to end, remember each other.

   Of these responses, which do you struggle with the most? Which do you believe is a strength you have?

4. When you back up and consider the entire letter of James, what does he say that best helps you develop vibrant, living faith?

5. In what ways are you becoming "wholly given to God as he is wholly given to you?"

 Memory Verse James 5:16

Therefore confess your sins to each other and pray for each other so that you may be healed. The prayer of a righteous man is powerful and effective.